greatasianfood

greatasianfood

The Australian Women's
Weekly
cookbooks

contents

modern **asian** cooking

The mortar and pestle, traditionally used for grinding spices in Asian cooking, have been replaced by the blender or food processor, high quality commercial curry pastes are easy to find, and you can buy noodles of all types at your local supermarket. Asian food has gone mainstream. Here are some tips to make cooking Asian at home even easier.

the rice **question**

Rice, in one form or another, is the cornerstone of all Asian meals. There are a number of different varieties of rice and several ways of cooking it, absorption and boiling being the most common. In almost all Asian countries, the absorption method is favoured since none of the rice's flavour or nutrients are lost – but choose the method that suits your needs best. Adding salt to the rice is also a matter of taste – in India, Sri Lanka and parts of Malaysia, salt is always added, but in the rest of Asia, it never is.

rice types

For an authentic Asian taste, you should choose the rice that is most appropriate for your particular dish.

long-grain long, slender grains that remain separate when cooked; most popular steaming rice in Asia.

jasmine lightly fragrant long-grain rice, that is much favoured in Thai cooking.

basmati aromatic, long-grain rice, popular in both India and Sri Lanka.

short-grain fat, almost round grains with a high starch content that makes them clump together when cooked; ideal for eating with chopsticks.

koshihikari small, round-grain white rice, perfect for Japanese food, especially sushi.

glutinous short-grain rice, either black or white, that becomes sticky and translucent when cooked; popular mostly for sweet desserts.

absorption method

Rinse uncooked rice until water runs clear. Combine water and rice in medium heavy-based saucepan. Cover tightly; bring to a boil. Reduce heat to as low as possible; cook 12-15 minutes. Do not remove lid during cooking. Remove pan from heat; stand, covered, 10 minutes. Fluff rice with a fork. An electric rice cooker also cooks by the absorption method. Often used in Asia and becoming increasingly more popular in non-Asian countries, a rice cooker is easy to use and gives consistently good results.

boiling method

Bring plenty of water to a boil in large saucepan; add rice. Stir to separate grains; boil, uncovered, about 12 minutes or until rice is tender, then drain and fluff with a fork. Do not rinse rice unless specified in recipe.

stir-fry be prepared

Since stir-frying takes so little time, all the ingredients must be prepared in advance. The preparation for a stir-fried recipe looks like a cookery demonstration on TV – sauces and stocks are prepared in advance, everything is sliced, chopped, grated, ready to go. The vegetables should be chopped into a uniform size and thickness. When you're ready to begin, heat the wok first, then add oil and cook the hardest-textured vegetables first (as they will take the longest to cook), adding leafy vegetables at the end of cooking time.

It is very important to make sure you don't crowd your wok. Cook in batches – especially meat or chicken – so that the food sizzles as it cooks. If there's too much in the wok, the food will stew rather than fry, making it tough.

spice of life

One of the greatest aids in cooking Asian food at home has been the proliferation of good quality readymade spice mixes and curry pastes that are now available. Use them by all means, since they can make life much easier, but if you have the time or inclination to make your own, you'll be delighted with the results. To save time, make a large batch of curry paste and freeze the excess in convenient portions for later use. If you are blending and storing spices however, be sure to prepare only small amounts, as ground spices rapidly lose their flavour and aroma.

using your **noodle**

There are almost as many noodle varieties as there are recipes to use them. Egg noodles and wheat noodles are the most common throughout Asia, but noodles are also made from rice flour, bean starch, buckwheat and numerous other forms of starch. Although we specify the type of noodle to use in particular recipes, feel free to substitute if that type of noodle is not available or if your family has a particular favourite.

seasoning your wok

Carbon steel and cast-iron woks (but not stainless steel and non-stick) must be "seasoned" before you use them. This is the method of ageing the wok so that food doesn't stick. The more you use your wok, the smoother and darker it will become and the less oil you'll need to use.

Firstly, wash the wok in hot soapy water to remove all traces of grease and lacquer (woks are sometimes coated in a thin film of lacquer to prevent their rusting

rice **quantities**		
quantity of rice	quantity of water	serves
1 cup (200g) long-grain	2 cups (500ml)	2
2 cups (400g) long-grain	3½ cups (875ml)	4
1 cup (200g) short/medium-grain	1½ cups (375ml)	2
2 cups (400g) short/medium-grain	2½ cups (625ml)	4

For long-grain rice, allow 1½ cups (375ml) water for every additional cup of rice; for short/medium-grain rice, allow 1 cup (250ml) for every additional cup of rice.

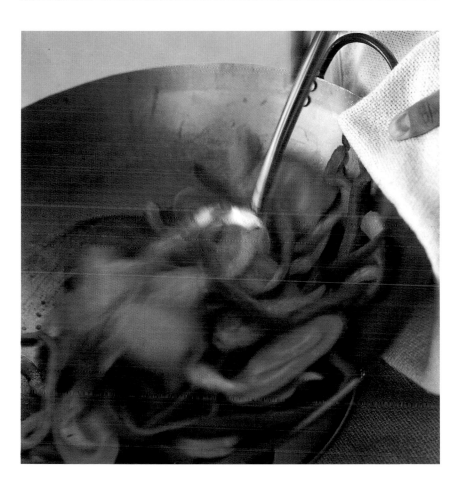

during shipping). Dry the wok thoroughly.

Place the wok on the stove over high heat; when hot, rub 1-2 tablespoons of peanut oil over the entire inside surface with absorbent paper. Wear oven gloves on both hands for this step as the oil and wok become very hot. Continue heating the wok for 10-15 minutes, wiping from time to time with a ball of clean absorbent paper. This will create a certain amount of smoke. Don't be alarmed – this is normal, because you are effectively "burning off" the oil on the surface of the wok. If you are worried about setting off your smoke alarm or filling the kitchen with smoke, season the wok outside on the barbecue.

Allow wok to cool completely, then repeat the heating and wiping process twice more (three times in all). Your wok is now ready to use. To wash the wok after cooking, use warm soapy water – no abrasives or scourers – and dry it well.

china

The food of China is as diverse as the country itself, with ingredients and cooking techniques depending on the origin of each dish. In the West, we're most at home with the familiar stir-fries of Cantonese cooking. But spicy Sichuan dishes and the robust hotpots and dumplings of the Peking region are rapidly gaining ground.

chicken
and corn soup

PREPARATION TIME 15 MINUTES ■ COOKING TIME 20 MINUTES

1.5 litres (6 cups) chicken stock

310g canned creamed corn

2/3 cup (130g) canned corn kernels, drained

1/2 teaspoon grated fresh ginger

1 teaspoon sesame oil

8 green onions, sliced thinly

1/4 cup (35g) cornflour

1/4 cup (60ml) water

2 egg whites

2 tablespoons water, extra

1 cup (170g) shredded cooked chicken

2 slices lean ham (80g), sliced thinly

1 Combine stock, creamed corn, corn kernels, ginger, oil and onion in large saucepan; bring to a boil.

2 Blend cornflour and the water in small jug; add to stock mixture. Cook, stirring, until mixture boils and thickens; reduce heat.

3 Combine egg whites and the extra water in small jug; add to soup in thin stream, stirring. Stir in chicken and ham; cook, uncovered, until heated through.

serves 6

per serving 4.5g fat; 894kJ

tips Soup can be made a day ahead and refrigerated, covered; reheat without boiling, when required.

Barbecued chicken or leftover roast chicken can be used for this soup. Homemade chicken stock, tetra packs, or stock cubes and water can be used.

sang choy bow

PREPARATION TIME 10 MINUTES ■ COOKING TIME 15 MINUTES

1 tablespoon vegetable oil

1 medium brown onion (150g), chopped finely

1 clove garlic, crushed

600g pork and veal mince

1 tablespoon soy sauce

1 tablespoon oyster sauce

250g bean sprouts, tips trimmed

200g fried noodles

3 green onions, sliced thinly

1 tablespoon white sesame seeds, toasted

8 large lettuce leaves

1 Heat oil in large saucepan; cook brown onion and garlic, stirring, until onion is soft. Add mince; cook, stirring, until mince is well browned.

2 Add combined sauces; simmer, uncovered, stirring occasionally, 5 minutes.

3 Just before serving, stir in sprouts, noodles, green onion and seeds. Divide mince mixture among lettuce leaves.

serves 4

per serving 23.2g fat; 1784kJ

tip We used crunchy dried noodles, sold in 100g cellophane bags, for this recipe.

wonton soup

PREPARATION TIME 30 MINUTES ▪ COOKING TIME 40 MINUTES

2 teaspoons peanut oil
2 cloves garlic, crushed
2 litres (8 cups) chicken stock
1 tablespoon soy sauce
1 litre (4 cups) water
4 green onions, sliced thinly

wontons
1 tablespoon peanut oil
4 green onions, sliced thinly
2 cloves garlic, crushed
1 tablespoon grated fresh ginger
400g minced pork
2 tablespoons soy sauce
36 wonton wrappers
1 egg, beaten lightly

1 Heat oil in large saucepan; cook garlic, stirring, 2 minutes. Stir in stock, sauce and the water; bring to a boil. Reduce heat; simmer, uncovered, 15 minutes. *[Can be made a day ahead to this stage; cool to room temperature then refrigerate, covered, or freeze for up to 3 months.]*

2 Just before serving, divide wontons among serving bowls. Pour over hot soup; sprinkle with onion.

wontons Heat oil in large frying pan; cook onion, garlic and ginger, stirring, until onion is soft. Add pork; cook, stirring, until pork is just browned. Stir in sauce. Place rounded teaspoons of cooled pork mixture in centre of each wrapper. Brush edges with egg; pinch edges together to seal. Repeat with remaining wrappers, pork mixture and egg. *[Can be made 3 hours ahead and refrigerated, covered, or frozen for up to a month.]*

serves 6

per serving 16.6g fat; 1980kJ
tips Gow gee wrappers can be substituted for wonton wrappers.
Wrap unused wonton wrappers in plastic and freeze for up to 2 months.

stir-fried asian
greens

PREPARATION TIME 10 MINUTES ■ COOKING TIME 10 MINUTES

1kg baby bok choy

500g choy sum

300g tat soi

1 tablespoon peanut oil

2 cloves garlic, crushed

2 teaspoons grated fresh ginger

1 tablespoon soy sauce

1 tablespoon oyster sauce

1 Cut off bottom of stems and any unsightly leaves on bok choy, choy sum and tat soi. Halve bok choy lengthways; separate leaves of other vegetables.

2 Heat oil in heated large wok or frying pan; stir-fry garlic and ginger until fragrant.

3 Add greens to wok; stir-fry, tossing, until just wilted.

4 Stir in sauces; toss gently until heated through.

serves 4

per serving 5.3g fat; 392kJ

steamed chicken
gow gees

PREPARATION TIME 40 MINUTES (plus refrigeration and standing time) ■ COOKING TIME 10 MINUTES

2 dried shiitake mushrooms

500g minced chicken

2 green onions, chopped finely

1 tablespoon finely chopped fresh garlic chives

2 cloves garlic, crushed

2 teaspoons grated fresh ginger

1/4 teaspoon five-spice powder

3/4 cup (75g) packaged breadcrumbs

2 tablespoons hoisin sauce

1 teaspoon sesame oil

1 egg, beaten lightly

30 gow gee wrappers

1 tablespoon chinese barbecue sauce

1 tablespoon light soy sauce

2 tablespoons water

2 teaspoons sweet chilli sauce

1 Place mushrooms in small heatproof bowl; cover with boiling water. Stand 20 minutes; drain. Discard stems; chop caps finely.

2 Combine mushrooms, chicken, onion, chives, garlic, ginger, five-spice, breadcrumbs, hoisin sauce, oil and egg in large bowl. Roll level tablespoons of chicken mixture into balls (you will have 30 balls); place on trays. Cover; refrigerate 30 minutes. *[Can be made a day ahead to this stage or frozen for up to a month.]*

3 Brush one wrapper with a little water; top with a chicken ball. Pleat wrapper firmly around ball. Repeat with remaining chicken balls and wrappers. Place gow gees in single layer, about 2cm apart, in baking-paper-lined bamboo steamer. Cook, covered, over large wok or frying pan of simmering water about 8 minutes or until gow gees are cooked through.

4 Combine remaining ingredients in small bowl. Serve as a dipping sauce with steamed gow gees.

makes 30

per gow gee 2g fat; 243kJ

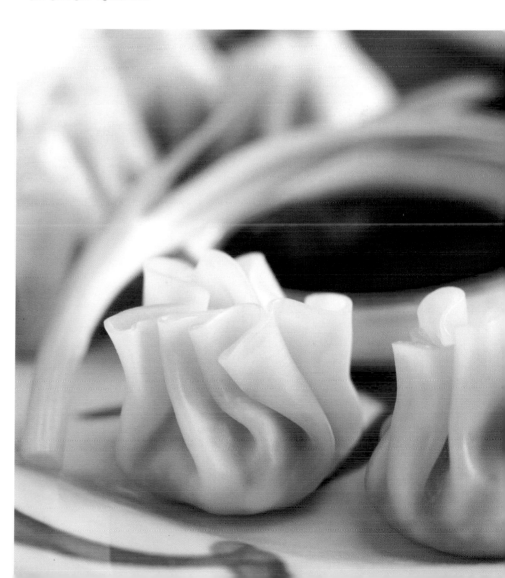

peking duck

PREPARATION TIME 2 HOURS 30 MINUTES (plus standing time) ■ 1 HOUR 10 MINUTES

2kg duck
¼ cup (60ml) honey, warmed
1 lebanese cucumber (130g)
8 green onions

pancakes
1½ cups (225g) plain flour
1½ teaspoons sugar
¾ cup (180ml) boiling water

sauce
⅓ cup (80ml) hoisin sauce
2 tablespoons chicken stock
1 tablespoon plum sauce

1 Wash duck; drain well. Tie string around neck of duck. Lower duck into large saucepan of boiling water for 20 seconds; remove from pan. Drain well; pat dry with absorbent paper. Tie string to refrigerator shelf and suspend duck, uncovered, over drip tray overnight. Remove duck from refrigerator; suspend duck in front of cold air from an electric fan about 2 hours or until skin is dry to touch.

2 Tuck wings under duck. Place duck, breast-side up, on wire rack in large baking dish; brush entire duck evenly with honey. Bake, uncovered, in moderate oven 30 minutes; turn duck. Reduce heat to slow; bake, uncovered, about 1 hour or until tender.

3 Place duck on chopping board; remove skin. Place skin in single layer on wire rack over oven tray; bake skin, uncovered, in moderate oven about 10 minutes or until crisp and browned. Slice skin; slice duck meat. Using teaspoon, remove seeds from cucumber. Cut cucumber and onions into thin 8cm strips. To serve, top warm pancakes with duck meat, crisp skin, cucumber, onion and sauce; roll. Eat with fingers.

pancakes Sift flour and sugar in large bowl; add the water. Stir quickly using wooden spoon until ingredients cling together. Knead dough on floured surface about 10 minutes or until smooth. Wrap dough in plastic; stand 30 minutes at room temperature. Divide dough into 16 pieces; roll one piece into a 16cm round. Heat small heavy-based frying pan; dry-fry pancake about 10 seconds on each side or until browned lightly. Repeat with remaining dough. Wrap pancakes in foil after each is cooked to prevent drying out. If necessary, pancakes can be reheated in bamboo steamer or microwave oven. Line steamer with cloth; place pancakes in single layer on cloth. Steam over simmering water about 2 minutes or until pancakes are heated through.

sauce Combine ingredients in small bowl; mix well.

serves 4

per serving 107.2g fat; 5935kJ
tips Duck must be prepared a day ahead and refrigerated, uncovered.
We used the more fleshy muscovy duck in this recipe. Cooked duck can also be purchased from Chinese barbecue shops and some restaurants.

prawn toasts

PREPARATION TIME 30 MINUTES ■ COOKING TIME 15 MINUTES

16 large uncooked prawns (800g)
2 eggs, beaten lightly
1/4 cup (35g) cornflour
8 thick slices white bread
1 green onion, chopped finely
vegetable oil, for deep-frying

sweet chilli dipping sauce
1/4 cup (60ml) sweet chilli sauce
1/4 cup (60ml) chicken stock
2 teaspoons soy sauce

1 Shell and devein prawns, leaving tails intact. Cut lengthways along backs of prawns, without separating halves. Toss flattened prawns in medium bowl with combined egg and cornflour; mix well.

2 Remove and discard crusts from bread; cut each slice in half. Place one prawn, cut-side down, on each piece of bread; gently flatten prawn onto bread. Sprinkle prawns with onion; press on firmly.

3 Heat oil in large wok or frying pan; carefully lower prawn toasts, in batches, into hot oil. Deep-fry until browned lightly and cooked through; drain on absorbent paper. Serve with sweet chilli dipping sauce.

sweet chilli dipping sauce Combine ingredients in small bowl.

makes 16

per prawn toast 5g fat;533kJ

mini spring rolls

PREPARATION TIME 35 MINUTES (plus standing time) ■ COOKING TIME 25 MINUTES

4 dried shiitake mushrooms

100g dried thin wheat noodles

1 clove garlic, crushed

1 teaspoon grated fresh ginger

4 green onions, sliced thinly

1/2 medium carrot (60g), sliced thinly

40g bean sprouts, tips trimmed

2 teaspoons oyster sauce

2 teaspoons cornflour

2 teaspoons water

24 x 12.5cm square spring roll wrappers

peanut oil, for deep-frying

chilli cucumber sauce

1 lebanese cucumber (130g), chopped finely

1/4 cup (60ml) sweet chilli sauce

1 small tomato (130g), peeled, seeded, chopped coarsely

1 teaspoon light soy sauce

1 clove garlic, crushed

1 Place mushrooms in small heatproof bowl; cover with boiling water. Stand 20 minutes; drain. Discard stems; slice caps thinly.

2 Cook noodles in large saucepan of boiling water, uncovered, until just tender; drain. Rinse under cold running water; drain. Cut noodles into 6cm lengths.

3 Combine mushrooms and noodles in large bowl with garlic, ginger, onion, carrot, sprouts and sauce. Blend cornflour with the water in small bowl.

4 Spoon 1 level tablespoon of noodle mixture across a corner of one wrapper. Lightly brush edges of wrapper with a little of the cornflour mixture; roll to enclose filling, folding in ends. Roll should be about 6cm long. Repeat with remaining noodle mixture, wrappers and cornflour mixture.

5 Just before serving, heat oil in large saucepan; deep-fry spring rolls, in batches, until golden brown and cooked through. Drain spring rolls on absorbent paper; serve with chilli cucumber sauce.

chilli cucumber sauce Reserve 1/4 cup cucumber. Blend or process remaining ingredients until smooth. Stir in reserved cucumber.

makes 24

per spring roll 1.4g fat; 164kJ

tips Filling and chilli cucumber sauce can be made 3 hours ahead and refrigerated, covered, separately.

Spring rolls can be prepared 30 minutes before deep-frying and refrigerated, covered with slightly damp tea-towel. Uncooked rolls suitable to freeze for up to 6 months.

crab
in black bean sauce

PREPARATION TIME 30 MINUTES (plus freezing time) ■ COOKING TIME 20 MINUTES

2 x 1.5kg uncooked mud crabs
1$1/2$ tablespoons packaged salted black beans
1 tablespoon peanut oil
1 clove garlic, crushed
1 teaspoon grated fresh ginger
$1/2$ teaspoon sambal oelek
1 tablespoon light soy sauce
1 teaspoon sugar
1 tablespoon chinese rice wine
$3/4$ cup (180ml) chicken stock
2 green onions, sliced lengthways

1 Place live crabs in freezer for at least 2 hours; this is the most humane way to kill a crab. Slide a sharp, strong knife under top of shell at back of each crab; lever off shell and discard.

2 Remove and discard gills; wash crabs thoroughly. Using cleaver, chop body into quarters. Remove claws and nippers; chop nippers into large pieces.

3 Rinse beans well under cold running water; drain. Lightly mash beans. Heat oil in heated large wok or frying pan; stir-fry garlic, ginger and sambal oelek until fragrant. Add beans, sauce, sugar, wine and stock; bring to a boil.

4 Add all of the crab; cook, covered, about 15 minutes or until crab changes colour. Place crab on serving plate; pour over sauce. Top with onion.

serves 4

per serving 7.1g fat; 1186kJ
tip Place green onion strips in iced water about 20 minutes to make onion curls, a classic Chinese garnish.

combination stir-fry

PREPARATION TIME 20 MINUTES ■ COOKING TIME 15 MINUTES

1 tablespoon peanut oil

500g chicken thigh fillets, chopped finely

250g minced pork

1 medium brown onion (150g), chopped finely

2 cloves garlic, crushed

2 teaspoons grated fresh ginger

1 large carrot (180g), chopped coarsely

500g medium uncooked prawns, shelled, deveined

300g chinese cabbage, shredded

425g can baby corn, drained

230g can sliced bamboo shoots, drained, chopped finely

80g bean sprouts, trimmed, chopped coarsely

2 green onions, chopped coarsely

1 teaspoon cornflour

2 tablespoons light soy sauce

1 tablespoon black bean sauce

1 Heat half of the oil in heated large wok or frying pan; stir-fry chicken, in batches, until browned and cooked through. Heat remaining oil in wok; stir-fry pork until browned. Add onion, garlic, ginger and carrot; stir-fry until onion is soft. Add prawns; stir-fry until prawns just change colour.

2 Return chicken to wok with remaining vegetables and blended cornflour and sauces; stir-fry until cabbage is wilted.

serves 4

per serving 19g fat; 1955kJ

honey prawns

PREPARATION TIME 30 MINUTES ■ COOKING TIME 15 MINUTES

1.5kg large uncooked prawns

1 cup (150g) self-raising flour

1¼ cups (310ml) water

1 egg, beaten lightly

cornflour

vegetable oil, for deep-frying

2 teaspoons peanut oil

¼ cup (60ml) honey

100g snow pea sprouts

2 tablespoons white sesame seeds, toasted

1 Shell and devein prawns, leaving tails intact. Place self-raising flour in medium bowl; gradually whisk in the water and egg until batter is smooth. Just before serving, coat prawns in cornflour; shake off excess. Dip prawns in batter, one at a time; drain off excess.

2 Heat vegetable oil in large wok or frying pan. Deep-fry prawns, in batches, until browned lightly; drain on absorbent paper.

3 Heat peanut oil in cleaned wok; heat honey, uncovered, until bubbling. Add prawns; coat with honey mixture. Serve prawns on sprouts; sprinkle with seeds.

serves 4

per serving 25.3g fat; 2765kJ

steamed gingered
snapper

PREPARATION TIME 10 MINUTES ■ COOKING TIME 40 MINUTES

40g piece fresh ginger
1 large whole snapper (1.2kg)
1/4 cup (60ml) vegetable stock
4 green onions, sliced thinly
1/2 cup tightly packed fresh coriander, chopped coarsely
1/3 cup (80ml) light soy sauce
1 teaspoon sesame oil

1 Peel ginger; cut into matchstick-sized pieces.

2 Score fish through the thickest part of flesh, on both sides; place on large sheet of oiled foil. Sprinkle with half of the ginger; drizzle with half of the stock. Fold foil loosely to enclose fish.

3 Place fish in large bamboo steamer; steam fish, covered, over large wok or frying pan of simmering water about 40 minutes or until cooked through.

4 Transfer fish to serving dish; sprinkle with remaining ginger, onion and coriander. Drizzle with combined remaining stock, sauce and oil.

serves 4

per serving 5.6g fat; 1224kJ

tip If snapper is unavailable, use your favourite whole firm-fleshed fish for this recipe.

lemon chicken

PREPARATION TIME 20 MINUTES (plus marinating time) ■ COOKING TIME 25 MINUTES

700g chicken breast fillets

1/3 cup (80ml) lemon juice

1 tablespoon brown sugar

1 tablespoon grated fresh ginger

2 cloves garlic, crushed

2 tablespoons peanut oil

250g dried thin egg noodles

1 medium brown onion (150g), sliced thinly

1 medium red capsicum (200g), sliced thinly

1 trimmed stick celery (75g), sliced thinly

4 green onions, sliced thinly

1/3 cup firmly packed fresh coriander

lemon sauce

1 teaspoon cornflour

2 teaspoons finely grated lemon rind

1/3 cup (80ml) lemon juice

2 cups (500ml) chicken stock

1/4 cup (60ml) honey

1 teaspoon sambal oelek

1 Cut chicken into thin, even slices; place in large bowl containing blended lemon juice, sugar, ginger, garlic and 1 tablespoon of the oil. Mix well to coat chicken in marinade. Cover; refrigerate 1 hour or until required. *[Can be made a day ahead to this stage or frozen for up to a month.]*

2 Just before serving, cook noodles in large saucepan of boiling water, uncovered, until just tender; drain.

3 Heat remaining oil in heated large wok or frying pan; stir-fry chicken mixture, in batches, until browned and almost cooked through. Add brown onion, capsicum, celery and green onion to wok; stir-fry over high heat until vegetables are just browned.

4 Return chicken mixture to wok. Add lemon sauce and noodles; stir-fry over high heat, tossing, until sauce mixture just boils and thickens slightly. Remove from heat; stir in coriander. Serve immediately.

lemon sauce Blend cornflour with rind and a little of the juice by whisking together in a small bowl or jug until smooth. Stir in remaining juice, stock, honey and sambal oelek; whisk to combine.

serves 4

per serving 19.7g fat; 2901kJ

chengdu-style duck

PREPARATION TIME 25 MINUTES (plus marinating time) ■ COOKING TIME 15 MINUTES

1 tablespoon finely chopped fresh
    lemon grass

1 tablespoon coarsely chopped
    fresh mint

2 cloves garlic, crushed

2 teaspoons sichuan peppercorns

2 teaspoons finely grated
    lemon rind

1/2 teaspoon hot paprika

600g duck breast fillets,
    sliced thinly

2 tablespoons cornflour

1 tablespoon peanut oil

400g baby bok choy, sliced thickly

120g bean sprouts, tips trimmed

1/4 cup (60ml) sweet chilli sauce

1 Using blender or mortar and pestle, make a paste of lemon grass, mint, garlic, peppercorns, rind and paprika.

2 Combine duck in large bowl with spice paste, cornflour and oil, mix well, cover; refrigerate 3 hours or until required. *[Can be made a day ahead to this stage or frozen for up to a month.]*

3 Stir-fry duck mixture in heated large wok or frying pan, in batches, until browned and cooked through.

4 Drain all but 1 tablespoon of fat from wok. Stir-fry bok choy and sprouts until just wilted.

5 Return duck mixture to wok with sauce; stir-fry, tossing to combine ingredients.

serves 4

per serving 60.7g fat; 2791kJ

fried rice

PREPARATION TIME 10 MINUTES ■ COOKING TIME 15 MINUTES

2 teaspoons peanut oil

2 eggs, beaten lightly

1 teaspoon sesame oil

4 bacon rashers (280g), chopped coarsely

1 medium brown onion (150g),
   chopped coarsely

2 trimmed sticks celery (150g),
   sliced thickly

1 clove garlic, crushed

1 tablespoon grated fresh ginger

3 cups (600g) cold, cooked, long-grain white rice

100g small cooked shelled prawns

425g can baby corn, drained, sliced thinly

1/2 cup (125g) frozen peas, thawed

4 green onions, sliced thinly

1 tablespoon soy sauce

1 Heat 1 teaspoon of the peanut oil in heated large wok or heavy-based frying pan. Add half of the egg; swirl wok to make a thin omelette. Remove omelette from wok. Roll omelette; cut into thin strips. Repeat with remaining egg.

2 Heat remaining peanut oil and sesame oil in wok; stir-fry bacon until brown. Add onion, celery, garlic and ginger; stir-fry over high heat until vegetables are just tender.

3 Add rice, omelette and remaining ingredients to wok; stir-fry, tossing, until well combined and heated through.

serves 4

per serving 10.8g fat; 1586kJ

hot and sour chicken

PREPARATION TIME 15 MINUTES (plus marinating time) ■ COOKING TIME 15 MINUTES

4 cloves garlic, crushed

2 tablespoons lemon pepper seasoning

4 red thai chillies, seeded, chopped finely

1/2 cup (125ml) water

2 tablespoons thick tamarind concentrate

1kg chicken breast fillets, sliced thinly

350g snake beans, trimmed

1 tablespoon peanut oil

2 large red onions (600g), sliced thickly

1 tablespoon sugar

1/4 cup (60ml) chicken stock

1 Combine garlic, seasoning, chilli, the water, tamarind and chicken in medium bowl. Cover; refrigerate 3 hours or until required. *[Can be made a day ahead to this stage or frozen for up to 3 months.]*

2 Boil, steam or microwave beans until just tender; drain.

3 Heat oil in heated large wok or frying pan; stir-fry chicken mixture and onion, in batches, until chicken is browned and cooked through.

4 Return chicken mixture to wok with beans, sugar and stock; stir-fry, tossing until sauce boils and thickens slightly.

serves 6

per serving 19.3g fat; 2043kJ

hot and sticky **ribs**

PREPARATION TIME 10 MINUTES ■ COOKING TIME 30 MINUTES

**1.5kg pork spareribs,
    chopped coarsely**

2 tablespoons peanut oil

2 cloves garlic, crushed

2 teaspoons grated fresh ginger

2 tablespoons honey

1/3 cup (80ml) sweet chilli sauce

2 tablespoons plum sauce

2 teaspoons sambal oelek

1 tablespoon brown sugar

**1 tablespoon finely chopped
    fresh coriander**

1 Cook spareribs in large saucepan of boiling water, uncovered, about
10 minutes or until just cooked. Drain spareribs; discard cooking liquid.

2 Heat oil in heated large wok or frying pan; stir-fry spareribs, in batches, until
browned and cooked as desired.

3 Return spareribs to wok with combined remaining ingredients; cook, stirring,
until sauce boils and thickens slightly.

serves 4

per serving 19.3g fat; 1741kJ

salt and pepper
squid

PREPARATION TIME 30 MINUTES ■ COOKING TIME 15 MINUTES

500g cleaned squid hoods
1/2 teaspoon cracked black pepper
1 teaspoon sea salt
1/2 teaspoon lemon pepper seasoning
1 tablespoon peanut oil

cucumber salad
1 lebanese cucumber (130g), sliced thinly
2 green onions, sliced thinly
250g cherry tomatoes, halved
1/3 cup (50g) roasted peanuts, chopped coarsely
1/2 cup fresh mint
1 tablespoon red wine vinegar
1 tablespoon peanut oil

1 Cut squid hoods along one side; open out. Score inside of hoods using sharp knife in diagonal pattern, without cutting all the way through – this will allow the squid to curl during cooking. *[Can be made a day ahead to this stage and refrigerated, covered.]*

2 Cut each squid hood into eight pieces. Sprinkle squid with combined pepper, salt and seasoning.

3 Heat oil in heated large wok or frying pan; stir-fry squid, in batches, until curled and just cooked through. Serve squid with cucumber salad.

cucumber salad Combine cucumber, onion, tomato, peanuts and mint in large bowl. Add combined vinegar and oil; mix gently.

serves 4

per serving 16.7g fat; 1108kJ
tip Squid hoods are suitable to freeze, but before doing so check with the fishmonger that they have not been frozen previously.

beef
and black bean stir-fry

PREPARATION TIME 20 MINUTES (plus marinating time) ■ COOKING TIME 15 MINUTES

500g beef round steak, sliced thinly

2 cloves garlic, crushed

2 teaspoons grated fresh ginger

2 tablespoons lime juice

1/2 teaspoon sugar

1 tablespoon peanut oil

**1 large brown onion (200g),
    sliced thickly**

400g broccoli florets

2 large carrots (360g), sliced thinly

1/3 cup (80ml) black bean sauce

1 tablespoon soy sauce

1 teaspoon cornflour

2 tablespoons water

2 teaspoons finely grated lime rind

1 Combine beef, garlic, ginger, juice and sugar in medium bowl; mix well. Cover; refrigerate 4 hours or until required. *[Can be made a day ahead to this stage or frozen for up to 3 months.]*

2 Heat half of the oil in heated large wok or frying pan; stir-fry beef mixture, in batches, until browned.

3 Heat remaining oil in wok; stir-fry onion, broccoli and carrot about 2 minutes or until vegetables are tender.

4 Return beef to wok. Add blended sauces, cornflour and the water; cook, stirring, about 2 minutes or until mixture boils and thickens slightly. Serve sprinkled with rind.

serves 4

per serving   11.9g fat; 1252kJ

wilted chinese greens with
pork

PREPARATION TIME 30 MINUTES ■ COOKING TIME 10 MINUTES

500g choy sum

350g chinese broccoli

500g baby bok choy

2 tablespoons peanut oil

**4 green onions, cut into
5cm lengths**

**200g fresh shiitake
mushrooms, quartered**

**500g chinese barbecued pork,
sliced thinly**

300g silken tofu, cubed

1 cup (100g) mung bean sprouts

macadamia dressing

**½ cup macadamias, toasted,
chopped finely**

½ cup (125ml) peanut oil

¼ cup (60ml) chinese rice wine

1 tablespoon soy sauce

⅓ cup (80ml) rice vinegar

1 Trim choy sum, broccoli and bok choy; chop coarsely.

2 Heat half of the oil in heated large wok or frying pan; stir-fry onion and mushrooms until mushrooms are just tender. Add pork; stir-fry 1 minute. Remove mixture from wok.

3 Heat remaining oil in wok; stir-fry choy sum, broccoli and bok choy until just wilted.

4 Gently toss pork mixture, vegetable mixture, tofu and sprouts in large bowl with macadamia dressing.

macadamia dressing Combine ingredients in screw-top jar; shake well.

serves 4

per serving 77.1g fat; 3797kJ

tip Ready-to-eat barbecued pork can be purchased from Asian barbecue stores and some restaurants.

noodles
with asparagus

PREPARATION TIME 15 MINUTES ■ COOKING TIME 10 MINUTES

450g hokkien noodles
1 teaspoon peanut oil
1/4 teaspoon chilli oil
2 cloves garlic, crushed
2 teaspoons finely grated fresh ginger
1 fresh red thai chilli, chopped finely
500g asparagus, trimmed, chopped into 3cm lengths
1 tablespoon salt-reduced soy sauce
1 tablespoon chinese barbecue sauce
2 teaspoons chinese rice wine
2 teaspoons cornflour
1/4 cup (60ml) chicken stock
4 green onions, sliced thickly
1/4 cup (30g) dried shrimp

1 Rinse noodles under hot running water; drain. Transfer to large bowl; separate noodles with fork.

2 Heat oils in heated large wok or frying pan. Add garlic, ginger and chilli; stir-fry until fragrant. Add asparagus; stir-fry until asparagus is just tender.

3 Add noodles, sauces, wine and blended cornflour and stock; stir until mixture boils and thickens slightly. Add onion and shrimp; stir until heated through.

serves 4

per serving 2.2g fat; 855kJ

mongolian
garlic lamb

PREPARATION TIME 20 MINUTES (plus marinating time) ■ COOKING TIME 20 MINUTES

1kg lamb fillets, cut into strips

1 teaspoon five-spice powder

2 teaspoons sugar

3 cloves garlic, crushed

1 egg, beaten lightly

1 tablespoon cornflour

1½ tablespoons rice wine vinegar

⅓ cup (80ml) soy sauce

1 tablespoon black bean sauce

¼ cup (60ml) peanut oil

**3 medium brown onions (450g),
    sliced thickly**

⅓ cup (80ml) beef stock

¼ teaspoon sesame oil

2 green onions, sliced thinly

1 Combine lamb in large bowl with five-spice, sugar, garlic and egg. Blend cornflour with vinegar and half of the combined sauces; stir into lamb mixture. Cover; refrigerate 1 hour. *[Can be made a day ahead to this stage.]*

2 Drain lamb over small bowl; reserve marinade. Heat half of the peanut oil in heated large wok or frying pan; stir-fry lamb mixture, in batches, until browned and almost cooked through. Heat remaining peanut oil in wok; stir-fry brown onion until soft.

3 Return lamb to wok with reserved marinade, remaining sauces, stock and sesame oil; cook, stirring, until mixture boils and thickens slightly. Serve sprinkled with green onion.

serves 4

per serving 25.3g fat; 2171kJ

five-spice chicken

PREPARATION TIME 20 MINUTES (plus marinating time) ■ COOKING TIME 25 MINUTES

**700g chicken breast fillets,
  sliced thinly**

1 teaspoon finely grated lime rind

2 tablespoons lime juice

2 cloves garlic, crushed

2 teaspoons grated fresh ginger

1 teaspoon five-spice powder

1/4 cup (60ml) soy sauce

2 tablespoons peanut oil

250g chinese cabbage, shredded

**11/2 cups (120g) bean sprouts,
  tips trimmed**

8 green onions, sliced thickly

**1/4 cup loosely packed
  fresh coriander**

1 Combine chicken, rind, juice, garlic, ginger, five-spice and 1 tablespoon of the sauce in large bowl. Cover; refrigerate 3 hours or until required. *[Can be made a day ahead to this stage or frozen for up to 3 months.]*

2 Heat half of the oil in heated large wok or frying pan; stir-fry chicken mixture, in batches, until chicken is browned and cooked through.

3 Heat remaining oil in wok; stir-fry cabbage, sprouts and onion until cabbage is just wilted.

4 Return chicken mixture to wok with coriander and remaining sauce; stir-fry, tossing to combine with vegetables. Serve with deep-fried rice noodles, if desired.

serves 4

per serving 18.9g fat; 1448kJ

asian nut mix

PREPARATION TIME 10 MINUTES (plus cooling time)
COOKING TIME 35 MINUTES

1½ cups (225g) unsalted raw cashews

1½ cups (150g) walnuts

2 teaspoons grated fresh ginger

1½ teaspoons mild sweet chilli sauce

2 cloves garlic, crushed

1 tablespoon salt-reduced soy sauce

1 Place cashews on oven tray. Bake in moderate oven about 15 minutes or until browned lightly; cool.

2 Combine cashews with remaining ingredients in large bowl. Spread nut mixture over greased oven tray. Bake in moderate oven, stirring occasionally, about 20 minutes or until crisp; cool.

makes 3 cups

per cup 71.6g fat; 325kJ

red curry fish cakes

PREPARATION TIME 45 MINUTES
COOKING TIME 15 MINUTES

1kg small white fish fillets, chopped coarsely

1 egg

2 teaspoons coarsely chopped fresh coriander

3 teaspoons sugar

⅓ cup (100g) red curry paste (recipe p 202)

100g green beans, sliced thinly

vegetable oil, for deep frying

1 Blend or process fish, egg, coriander, sugar and paste until well combined and smooth.

2 Combine fish mixture and beans in large bowl; mix well.

3 Roll 2 level tablespoons of mixture into a ball, flatten slightly; repeat with remaining mixture.

4 Heat oil in large wok or frying pan. Deep-fry fish cakes, in batches, until well browned and cooked through; drain on absorbent paper.

makes 25

per fish cake 7g fat; 424kJ
tips Fish cakes can be made a day ahead and refrigerated, covered, or frozen for up to a month. We used redfish fillets for this recipe.

lemon ginger prawns

PREPARATION TIME 15 MINUTES (plus marinating time)
COOKING TIME 10 MINUTES

30 uncooked king prawns (about 1kg)
2 teaspoons lemon juice
2 teaspoons grated fresh ginger
1 tablespoon light soy sauce
1 teaspoon sesame oil
pinch five-spice powder
2 tablespoons olive oil

1 Shell and devein prawns, leaving tails intact.
Combine juice, ginger, sauce, sesame oil
and spice in large bowl; stir in prawns.
Cover; refrigerate 1 hour. *[Can be made a
day ahead to this stage.]*

2 Just before serving, thread prawns onto
30 skewers. Heat oil in large frying pan;
cook skewers until tender.

makes 30

per skewer 1.5g fat; 115kJ
tip Soak bamboo skewers in water about 1 hour to
prevent them from burning.

sesame chicken toasts

PREPARATION TIME 20 MINUTES
COOKING TIME 15 MINUTES

250g chicken mince
1 clove garlic, crushed
**1 tablespoon finely chopped
   fresh coriander**
1 tablespoon sweet chilli sauce
6 thick slices white bread
1/3 cup (50g) white sesame seeds
vegetable oil, for deep-frying

1 Combine chicken, garlic, coriander and
sauce in small bowl. Remove crusts from
bread; spread chicken mixture over one side
of each bread slice. Dip bread, chicken-side
down, in sesame seeds to coat.

2 Just before serving, heat oil in heated large
wok or frying pan. Deep-fry bread, two
pieces at a time, until well browned; drain on
absorbent paper. Cut each piece of toast into
quarters to serve.

makes 24 triangles

per triangle 4.4g fat; 384kJ

japan

With its freshness, simplicity and beautiful presentation,
Japanese food is as much a feast for the eye as it is for the palate.
Very few seasonings are used, allowing the pure flavour and
quality of the ingredients themselves to predominate.
Indeed, Japanese food has everything the modern cook wants:
it's easy and mostly quick to prepare, very low in fat – and delicious.

miso soup
with pork and beans

PREPARATION TIME 15 MINUTES ■ COOKING TIME 10 MINUTES

1 litre (4 cups) dashi stock

100g pork fillet, sliced thinly

8 green beans, cut into 2cm lengths

1/4 cup (75g) red miso paste (karakuchi)

2 teaspoons ginger juice

2 green onions, sliced thinly

1 Bring stock to a boil in medium saucepan. Add pork and beans; return to a boil. Reduce heat; simmer, uncovered, 2 minutes.

2 Place miso in small bowl; gradually add 1 cup (250ml) of the hot stock, stirring until miso dissolves. Add to saucepan; stir to combine. Bring to a boil; remove from heat immediately.

3 Divide soup among serving bowls; stir 1/2 teaspoon of the juice into each bowl. Just before serving, sprinkle with onion.

serves 4

per serving 1.9g fat; 283kJ

tips Ginger juice can be squeezed from grated green ginger or extracted by squeezing some coarsely chopped green ginger through a garlic crusher. You will need about 2 tablespoons grated ginger to make 2 teaspoons ginger juice.

Do not overcook soup after miso is added or flavour will be lost.

beef and rice
soup

PREPARATION TIME 10 MINUTES ■ COOKING TIME 10 MINUTES

1.25 litres (5 cups) dashi stock

3 teaspoons light soy sauce

3 cups (600g) hot cooked koshihikari rice

150g lean beef fillet, cut into paper-thin slices

2 teaspoons toasted white sesame seeds

2 green onions, sliced thinly

2 teaspoons wasabi paste

1 Bring stock and sauce to a boil in medium saucepan.

2 Divide rice among serving bowls. Arrange beef, seeds and onion on top of rice. Divide soup among serving bowls, taking care not to dislodge the arrangement.

3 Serve soup immediately with wasabi in individual dishes.

serves 4

per serving 3.4g fat; 1071kJ

tips Beef is easier to slice thinly if placed in plastic wrap, in freezer, about 1 hour.

Beef will cook in the stock if sliced very thinly. You can brown unsliced beef in medium non-stick frying pan to add extra flavour to soup, if desired.

A medium-grain white rice can be substituted for koshihikari, if unavailable. White fish fillets can be substituted for beef, and seven-spice mix (shichimi togarashi) or chilli can be substituted for wasabi. Green tea is sometimes used as the broth instead of dashi.

sushi rice

PREPARATION TIME 10 MINUTES (plus draining time) ■ COOKING TIME 12 MINUTES (plus standing time)

3 cups (600g) uncooked short-grain white rice
3 cups (750ml) water

sushi vinegar
1/2 cup (125ml) rice vinegar (su)
1/4 cup (55g) sugar
1/2 teaspoon salt

1 Place rice in large bowl; fill with cold water. Stir with hand; drain. Repeat process two or three times until water is nearly clear; drain rice in strainer or colander at least 30 minutes.

2 Place drained rice in medium saucepan with the water; cover. Bring to a boil; reduce heat. Simmer, covered, on low heat about 12 minutes or until water is absorbed. Remove from heat; allow rice to stand, covered, 10 minutes.

3 Spread rice in large, non-metallic flat-bottomed bowl or tub (preferably wood). Using rice paddle or plastic spatula, repeatedly slice through rice at a sharp angle to break up any lumps and separate grains. Gradually pour in sushi vinegar at the same time. Not all of the vinegar may be required; the rice shouldn't become too wet or mushy.

4 Continue to slice rice (don't stir because it crushes the rice grains) with one hand, lifting and turning rice from the outside into the centre.

5 Meanwhile, using other hand, fan rice about 5 minutes or until almost cool; do not over-cool rice or it will harden. Performing these two actions together will give you glossy, slightly sticky but still separate sushi rice. Keep rice covered with damp cloth to stop it drying out while making sushi.

sushi vinegar Stir combined vinegar, sugar and salt in small bowl until sugar dissolves. To make this mixture slightly less stringent, heat gently just before using.

makes 9 cups

per cup 0.3g fat; 1086kJ
tips The success of sushi largely depends on perfectly cooked, cooled, vinegared rice (sumeshi). Use a short-grain rice such as koshihikari, if possible. Only short grain has the right texture and consistency to just stick together without being gluggy.
Add a little mirin or sake to the sushi vinegar mixture if desired, or use 1/2 cup (125ml) ready-made bottled sushi vinegar. Sushi vinegar can be made ahead and refrigerated in an airtight container.

sushi hand-rolls

PREPARATION TIME 30 MINUTES

**3 cups sushi rice
(see recipe page 46)**

**4 sheets toasted seaweed
(yaki-nori)**

1 large avocado (320g)

1 tablespoon lemon juice

2 tablespoons mayonnaise

1 teaspoon wasabi paste

**4 japanese seafood sticks,
quartered lengthways**

**1 lebanese cucumber (130g),
halved, seeded, cut lengthways
into 16 strips**

**1 teaspoon toasted black
sesame seeds**

½ cup (125ml) japanese soy sauce

**2 tablespoons pink pickled
ginger (gari)**

1 Place sushi rice in non-metallic serving bowl; cover with damp cloth. Cut each sheet of seaweed into quarters; cover with plastic wrap until ready to serve (seaweed must be kept covered because it softens and wrinkles if left exposed to the moisture in the air). Slice avocado thinly. Brush with lemon juice to stop it discolouring; cover. Combine mayonnaise and wasabi in small bowl; cover.

2 For each roll: place a quarter sheet of seaweed, shiny-side down, diagonally across palm of left hand, then dip fingers of right hand in small bowl of vinegared water. Shaking off excess water, pick up about 2 tablespoons of the rice; place in centre of seaweed. Using fingers of right hand, "rake" rice towards top corner of seaweed; make a slight groove down the middle of rice for filling.

3 Using one finger of right hand, swipe a dab of wasabi mayonnaise along the groove in rice; top with a slice each of avocado, seafood stick and cucumber then a small sprinkle of sesame seeds.

4 Fold one side of seaweed over to stick to rice; fold other side of seaweed over the first to form a cone. Tip of cone can be folded back to hold cone shape securely.

5 Dip hand-roll in sauce; top with a slice of ginger, if desired. Eat immediately.

makes 16 hand-rolls

per serving 5g fat; 667kJ

tips Hand-rolls can be made with half sheets of toasted seaweed, if preferred.

suggestions for alternative fillings

■ Cucumber, smoked salmon, avocado and fresh dill tips

■ Shelled cooked prawns, pickled daikon, snow pea sprouts and green onion

■ Sashimi tuna, salmon roe, avocado, shredded lettuce and cucumber

■ Sashimi salmon, wasabi mayonnaise, green onion and cooked asparagus

■ Shredded carrot, avocado, green onion, snow pea sprouts and japanese omelette

dashi broth

PREPARATION TIME 5 MINUTES (plus standing time) ■ COOKING TIME 15 MINUTES

100g somen noodles

3 dried shiitake mushrooms

1 lemon

2 teaspoons dashi granules

1.5 litres (6 cups) water

2 tablespoons cooking sake

2 tablespoons mirin

2 tablespoons japanese soy sauce

1 Cook noodles in medium saucepan of boiling water, uncovered, until just tender; drain.

2 Meanwhile, place mushrooms in small heatproof bowl; cover with boiling water. Stand 20 minutes; drain. Discard stems; slice caps thinly.

3 Using vegetable peeler, remove lemon peel in long wide pieces; cut pieces into very thin strips.

4 Combine remaining ingredients in large saucepan; bring to a boil. Reduce heat; simmer, uncovered, 10 minutes.

5 Just before serving, divide noodles, mushrooms and lemon among serving bowls; ladle hot broth into each bowl.

serves 6

per serving 0.2g fat; 360kJ

tip A few sliced snow peas or green beans; finely grated daikon or kumara; fresh shiitake mushrooms; shaved dried seaweed (wakame or konbu); or bean sprouts and tofu can be added to broth, if desired.

tuna sashimi

PREPARATION TIME 10 MINUTES (plus soaking time)

3/4 **cup (200g) finely shredded daikon**

400g block-size piece sashimi tuna (maguro), about 7cm across x 4cm high

2 teaspoons wasabi paste

2 tablespoons pink pickled ginger (gari)

ponzu sauce

1/4 **cup (60ml) lemon juice**

1/4 **cup (60ml) japanese soy sauce**

1/4 **cup (60ml) water or dashi stock**

1/2 **cup (120g) grated daikon**

1 Soak daikon in medium bowl of iced water 15 minutes; drain well.

2 Place tuna on chopping board; using very sharp knife, cut 6mm slices at right angles to the grain of the fish, holding the piece of skinned fish with your fingers and slicing with knife almost horizontal to the board.

3 Divide tuna slices among serving plates; mound equal amounts of daikon next to tuna.

4 Garnish plates with equal amounts of mounded wasabi and ginger; serve with separate bowl of ponzu sauce.

ponzu sauce Combine juice, sauce and the water in medium bowl. Squeeze excess liquid from daikon; shape into a small mound. Place in small dish. *[Unused sauce can be refrigerated 6 months.]*

serves 4

per serving 6.3g fat; 775kJ

tips The fish to use for sashimi and sushi should be fish that are in season and labelled "sashimi quality" as a guarantee of correct health and handling standards. This fish should have a firm texture, a pleasant sea-smell (but not "fishy"), bright red gills and bright, clear eyes (although this last is not an indication on its own because the eyes can sometimes be clouded). Either buy whole fish and fillet it yourself, or select fillets or blocks (of tuna) which can then be sliced for you by the fishmonger, if preferred. Fish slices change colour quickly once cut, so it is preferable to slice it as close to serving time as possible. Incidentally, meat from the same tuna can be three different shades of red or pink, depending on which part of the fish it is from.

If you choose to cut the fish for your sashimi or sushi yourself, always use a very sharp knife with a long, flexible, very thin blade. Never "saw" the fish but cut it in a single movement, pulling knife down and forward.

pot stickers

PREPARATION TIME 20 MINUTES (plus refrigeration time) ■ COOKING TIME 10 MINUTES

300g minced pork

2 tablespoons japanese soy sauce

pinch white pepper

1 teaspoon sugar

1 tablespoon sake

1 egg, beaten lightly

2 teaspoons sesame oil

350g cabbage, chopped finely

4 green onions, chopped finely

30 gow gee wrappers

1 tablespoon vegetable oil

1 Combine pork in medium bowl with sauce, pepper, sugar, sake, egg, sesame oil, cabbage and onion. Refrigerate mixture 1 hour.

2 Wet edge of one side of each wrapper. Place about 2 teaspoons of the pork mixture in centre of each wrapper; pleat damp side of wrapper only. Pinch both sides together to seal.

3 Cover base of large frying pan with water; bring to a boil. Place pouches in pan; reduce heat. Simmer, covered, 3 minutes. Using slotted spoon, remove pouches from pan; drain. Dry pan.

4 Heat vegetable oil in pan; cook pouches, one side and base only, until golden.

makes 30

per pot sticker 1.8g fat; 161kJ

tips Add chopped prawns, cheese, capsicum or scrambled egg to filling, if desired. Serve with a mixture of soy sauce and chilli oil, soy sauce and rice vinegar or ponzu sauce (see page 50).

sweet soy beef

PREPARATION TIME 10 MINUTES ■ COOKING TIME 10 MINUTES

200g gelatinous noodles (shirataki)

¹/₂ cup (125ml) japanese soy sauce

1 tablespoon sugar

**¹/₄ cup (60ml) mirin or sweet
  white wine**

**300g beef eye fillet, sliced
  paper thin**

**2 green onions, sliced diagonally
  into 2cm lengths**

2 teaspoons ginger juice

**5 cups (750g) hot cooked
  koshihikari rice**

1 Place noodles in medium saucepan of boiling water; bring to a boil. Cook 1 minute, separating noodles with chopsticks. Drain; cut into 10cm lengths.

2 Bring sauce, sugar and mirin to a boil in medium saucepan. Add beef; return to a boil. Reduce heat; simmer, stirring occasionally, until beef just changes colour. Strain beef over medium heatproof bowl; return sauce to pan.

3 Add onion and noodles; simmer about 3 minutes or until onion softens. Return beef to pan. Add juice; heat through.

4 Divide rice among serving bowls. Top rice with beef mixture and approximately ¹/₄ cup (60ml) of the sauce.

serves 4

per serving 7.1g fat; 1899kJ
tips You will need 2 cups (400g) uncooked rice to make 5 cups (750g) hot cooked rice.
The ginger juice is optional; you will need about 2 tablespoons grated fresh ginger to make 2 teaspoons ginger juice.
Beef is easier to slice if placed in plastic wrap, in freezer, about 1 hour.
Rice or cellophane noodles (harusame) can be substituted for shirataki, if preferred.

shabu-shabu

PREPARATION TIME 20 MINUTES ■ COOKING TIME 10 MINUTES

400g gelatinous noodles (shirataki), drained

300g firm tofu

12 fresh shiitake mushrooms

600g beef eye fillet, sliced thinly

4 small leeks (800g), washed, sliced diagonally into 2cm pieces

6 chinese cabbage leaves, chopped coarsely

100g bamboo shoots, sliced thinly

12 small pieces of decorative wheat gluten (fu)

1 quantity ponzu sauce (see page 50)

1/2 cup (120g) red maple radish (momiji oroshi) or finely grated daikon, drained well

4 green onions, chopped finely

10cm-long piece dried kelp (konbu), cut into 4 pieces

1.5 litres (6 cups) water or dashi stock

red maple radish (momiji oroshi)

6cm-long 5cm-diameter piece daikon (120g), peeled

4 hot dried red chillies

1 Rinse noodles under hot running water; drain. Cut into 20cm lengths.

2 Press tofu between two chopping boards with a weight on top; raise one end. Stand 25 minutes; cut into 2cm cubes.

3 Remove and discard mushroom stems; cut a cross in the top of each cap. Arrange beef, tofu, vegetables and wheat gluten on platter.

4 Divide ponzu sauce, radish and onion among individual serving bowls.

5 Make a few cuts along the edges of kelp to release flavour. Place in 2-litre (8 cup) flameproof casserole dish or pot with 1.125 litres (4 1/2 cups) of the water; bring to a boil. Remove konbu just before the water boils. Reduce heat; simmer 4 minutes.

6 Add a selection of ingredients to the broth. As soon as they are cooked, remove and dip meat and vegetables in ponzu sauce. Add more ingredients and extra broth or water as required. Skim the surface of broth periodically to remove scum.

red maple radish (momiji oroshi) Using a chopstick, poke four holes in one end of daikon. Seed chillies and push into each hole with chopstick. Grate the daikon and chillies in a circular motion with a Japanese or fine-toothed grater. Squeeze out excess liquid. Shape into small mounds and place in individual serving dishes or in the centre of ponzu sauce.

serves 4

per serving 23.5g fat; 2558kJ

tips When all the meat and vegetables are eaten, the broth can be drunk from cups with added noodles or rice.

spinach
with roasted sesame dressing

PREPARATION TIME 5 MINUTES ■ COOKING TIME 15 MINUTES

$^1/_3$ **cup (50g) white sesame seeds**

1 teaspoon sugar

**1$^1/_2$ tablespoons japanese
    soy sauce**

$^1/_4$ **cup (60ml) dashi stock**

600g spinach, trimmed

1 Toast seeds in heated small frying pan, without oil, shaking pan constantly until browned lightly and seeds begin to pop. Remove from heat; reserve 1 teaspoon for garnish. Blend, process or grind hot seeds until smooth. Combine ground seeds with sugar, sauce and dashi in screw-top jar; shake well until sugar dissolves.

2 Wash spinach well. Bring large saucepan of water to a boil; immerse spinach. Drain immediately; rinse under cold running water to stop cooking and retain colour. Wrap spinach leaves in bamboo mat. Roll firmly; gently squeeze out excess water. Cut spinach into 3cm lengths; arrange on serving plate.

3 Just before serving, pour dressing over spinach. Serve at room temperature, sprinkled with reserved sesame seeds.

serves 4

per serving 7.2g fat; 387kJ

tips Beans or watercress can be substituted for spinach and peanuts or macadamia nuts can be substituted for sesame seeds. You could even use tahini (sesame seed paste) instead of grinding the toasted sesame seeds. Garnish cooked spinach with smoked dried bonito flakes (katsuobushi), if desired.

soba in broth

PREPARATION TIME 10 MINUTES ■ COOKING TIME 15 MINUTES

200g dried soba

3 cups (750ml) dashi stock

¼ cup (60ml) japanese soy sauce

2 tablespoons mirin

1 teaspoon sugar

1 tablespoon vegetable oil

400g chicken breast fillet, sliced thinly

2 medium leeks (700g), sliced thinly

¼ teaspoon seven-spice mix (shichimi togarashi)

1 Cook noodles in large saucepan of boiling water, uncovered, until just tender. Drain; cover to keep warm.

2 Combine stock, 2 tablespoons of the sauce, half of the mirin and half of the sugar in medium saucepan; bring to a boil. Remove from heat; cover to keep hot.

3 Heat oil in medium frying pan; cook chicken and leek, stirring, until chicken is just cooked. Stir in remaining sauce, mirin and sugar; bring to a boil.

4 Divide noodles evenly among serving bowls; top with chicken mixture. Cover with broth; sprinkle with seven-spice mix.

serves 4

per serving 11.2g fat; 1648kJ

tip Add 1 tablespoon finely grated fresh ginger to broth for extra flavour.

teppanyaki

PREPARATION TIME 20 MINUTES (plus marinating time) ■ COOKING TIME 20 MINUTES

4 large uncooked prawns (200g)

2 cloves garlic, crushed

1/4 cup (60ml) japanese soy sauce

1 red thai chilli, seeded, chopped finely

350g chicken breast fillets, skin on, cut into 5cm pieces

500g beef eye fillet, sliced thinly

4 shiitake mushrooms

1 medium brown onion (150g), sliced thinly

50g snow peas, trimmed

1 medium red capsicum (200g), seeded, chopped coarsely

4 green onions, sliced thinly

dipping sauce

1/2 cup (125ml) japanese soy sauce

1 tablespoon mirin

1 tablespoon brown sugar

1 tablespoon finely grated fresh ginger

1/2 teaspoon sesame oil

1 Shell and devein prawns, leaving tails intact. Combine garlic, soy sauce and chilli in medium bowl; add prawns, chicken and beef, stand 20 minutes. Drain, discard marinade.

2 Remove and discard mushroom stems; cut a cross in the top of each cap. Arrange ingredients, except green onion, on serving platter.

3 Cook a selection of the ingredients on heated oiled grill plate (or grill or barbecue) until vegetables are just tender, prawns and beef are cooked as desired and chicken is cooked through.

4 Continue cooking remaining ingredients throughout the meal. Serve with green onion and individual bowls of dipping sauce.

dipping sauce Combine ingredients in medium saucepan; cook, stirring, until sugar dissolves. Divide sauce among individual serving bowls.

serves 4

per serving 15.9g fat; 1701kJ

tips Temperature can be lowered to medium once cooking has begun. None of the ingredients should take longer than 8 minutes to cook, so be careful not to overcook. Beef rump or sirloin steak can be substituted for eye fillet, if preferred.

whiting **tempura**

PREPARATION TIME 10 MINUTES ■ COOKING TIME 15 MINUTES

1 egg
¾ cup (180ml) iced water
½ cup (75g) plain flour
½ cup (75g) cornflour
vegetable oil, for deep-frying
12 whiting fillets (840g)
¼ cup (60ml) japanese soy sauce
2 tablespoons sweet chilli sauce
2 tablespoons water
1 tablespoon lemon juice
2 green onions, sliced thinly

1 Just before serving, whisk egg and the water together in medium bowl; stir in sifted flours all at once. Do not over-mix; the mixture should be lumpy.

2 Heat oil in large wok or frying pan. Dip fish fillets, one at a time, in batter; deep-fry, in batches, in hot oil, until browned lightly and just cooked through.

3 Drain fish on absorbent paper; serve immediately, or place in slow oven to keep warm while cooking remaining batches.

4 Serve fish with combined sauces, water, juice and onion.

serves 4

per serving 19.1g fat; 2042kJ
tip If serving whiting tempura as finger food, cut fish fillets into bite-sized pieces before coating with batter.

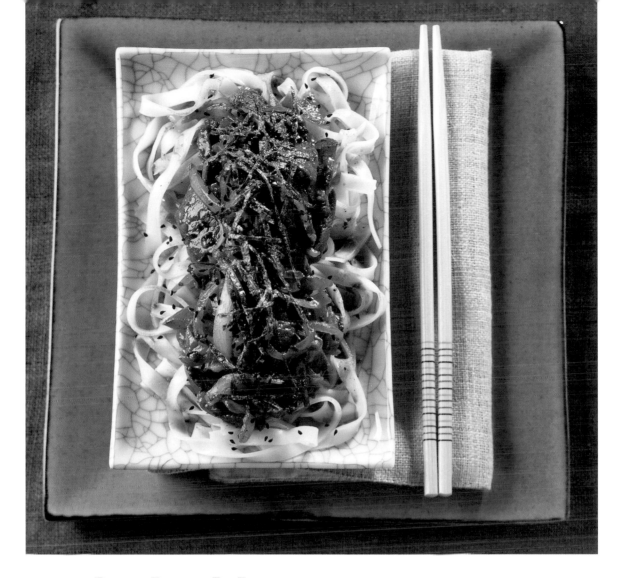

beef **teriyaki**

PREPARATION TIME 20 MINUTES (plus marinating time) ■ COOKING TIME 10 MINUTES

700g beef fillet, sliced thinly

¹/₄ cup (60ml) mirin

¹/₄ cup (60ml) ketjap manis

1 tablespoon rice vinegar

1 tablespoon finely chopped palm sugar

¹/₄ cup (60ml) lime juice

2 cloves garlic, crushed

3 fresh red thai chillies, seeded, chopped finely

1 tablespoon coarsely chopped glacé ginger

2 teaspoons sesame oil

375g rice stick noodles

2 tablespoons peanut oil

3 small red onions (300g), sliced thinly

2 tablespoons black sesame seeds

2 sheets toasted seaweed (yaki-nori), shredded

1 Combine beef, mirin, ketjap manis, vinegar, sugar, juice, garlic, chilli, ginger and sesame oil in large bowl. Cover; refrigerate 3 hours or until required. *[Can be made a day ahead to this stage and refrigerated, covered, or frozen for up to a month.]*

2 Place noodles in medium heatproof bowl. Cover with boiling water; stand until just tender. Drain; keep noodles warm. Drain beef over medium bowl; reserve marinade.

3 Heat peanut oil in heated large wok or frying pan; stir-fry beef and onion, in batches, until browned. Return beef to wok with reserved marinade; stir-fry until sauce boils.

4 Serve noodles topped with beef mixture; sprinkle with sesame seeds and seaweed.

serves 4

per serving 24.2g fat; 2979kJ

vegetable tempura

PREPARATION TIME 20 MINUTES ▨ COOKING TIME 20 MINUTES

250g firm tofu

1 medium brown onion (150g)

1 small fresh or frozen lotus root (200g)

8 fresh shiitake mushrooms

2 sheets toasted seaweed (yaki-nori)

20g cellophane noodles (harusame), cut in half

vegetable oil, for deep-frying

flour, for dusting ingredients

120g pumpkin, sliced thinly

50g green beans, halved

1 small kumara (250g), sliced thinly

1 baby eggplant, (60g) sliced thinly

1 small red capsicum (150g), seeded, cut into squares

1 medium carrot (120g), sliced thinly, diagonally

1 lemon, cut into wedges

batter

1 egg, beaten lightly

2 cups (500ml) iced soda water

1 cup (150g) plain flour

1 cup (150g) cornflour

dipping sauce

1 cup (250ml) dashi stock

1/3 cup (80ml) mirin

1/3 cup (80ml) light soy sauce

1/2 cup (120g) finely grated daikon, drained well

3 teaspoons grated fresh ginger

1 Press tofu between two chopping boards with a weight on top; raise one end. Stand 25 minutes; cut into 2cm cubes.

2 Halve onion from root end. Insert toothpicks at regular intervals to hold onion rings together; slice between toothpicks.

3 Peel lotus root; slice. Place in water with a dash of vinegar to prevent browning. If using canned lotus, drain and slice. Remove and discard mushroom stems; cut a cross in the top of each cap.

4 Cut one sheet seaweed into 5cm squares. Halve the other sheet; cut into 2cm-wide strips. Brush strips of seaweed with water; wrap tightly around about 10 noodles, either at one end or in the middle. Reserve noodle bunches.

5 Heat oil to moderately hot (170°C). Dust ingredients, except seaweed squares and lemon, lightly in flour, shaking off excess. Dip seaweed squares and other ingredients in batter; drain excess. Deep-fry ingredients, in batches, until golden; drain on paper towel. Only fry small amounts at a time and make sure enough time is allowed for oil to come back to correct temperature before adding next batch.

6 Finally, deep-fry noodle bundles; serve as a garnish.

7 Serve immediately with lemon wedges and individual bowls of warm dipping sauce.

batter Combine egg in medium bowl with the water. Add sifted flour all at once, mixing lightly until just combined, but still very lumpy.

dipping sauce Combine dashi, mirin and sauce in medium saucepan; heat gently. Divide among four individual serving bowls. Shape daikon into four pyramid shapes. Place a pyramid in each serving bowl; top with even amounts of ginger.

serves 4

per serving 37.1g fat; 3378kJ

tips Adjust the size or thickness of slower cooking vegetables (such as sweet potato and pumpkin) to ensure they cook at the same rate as faster cooking vegetables (such as zucchini). Always use fresh, clean oil and keep at a constant temperature during cooking. Optimum temperature for vegetables is fairly hot, about 170°C. For seafood, usually cooked after vegetables, the temperature should be slightly higher.

bean-curd pouches
with wasabi

PREPARATION TIME 35 MINUTES (plus refrigeration time)

80g bean thread noodles

1/3 cup (80ml) seasoned rice vinegar

10 green onions

10 pouches prepared fried bean curd

1/2 lebanese cucumber (65g), cut into matchstick-sized pieces

30g pickled ginger (gai), drained

2 teaspoons wasabi paste

1/4 cup (60ml) peanut oil

1/4 teaspoon sesame oil

1 teaspoon japanese soy sauce

1/2 teaspoon sugar

1 Place noodles in large heatproof bowl; cover with boiling water. Stand until just tender; drain. Rinse under cold running water; drain. Return noodles to bowl; stir in half of the vinegar. Line tray with plastic wrap; spread noodles on tray. Cover; refrigerate until cold.

2 Meanwhile, cut green tops from onions to measure about 26cm in length. Place tops in small heatproof bowl; cover with boiling water. Stand 5 minutes; drain. Rinse under cold running water; drain.

3 Gently open out pouches. Divide noodles among pouches; top with cucumber, ginger and half of the wasabi.

4 Tie onion tops around pouches to secure filling; trim ends of onion tops. Serve pouches with combined remaining vinegar and wasabi, oils, sauce and sugar.

makes 10

per pouch 11.8g fat; 705kJ

tip Recipe can be made a day ahead and refrigerated, covered.

beef and vegetable rolls

PREPARATION TIME 10 MINUTES ■ COOKING TIME 15 MINUTES

2 medium carrots (240g)

**6 asparagus spears,
    halved lengthways**

3 green onions

12 thin slices beef eye fillet (300g)

2 tablespoons cornflour

1 tablespoon vegetable oil

1 tablespoon sugar

**1/4 cup (60ml) mirin or sweet
    rice wine**

2 tablespoons sake

1/4 cup (60ml) japanese soy sauce

50g snow pea sprouts

1 Using vegetable peeler, shave carrot lengthways into narrow strips. Cut carrot strips to same width as beef. Place asparagus in heatproof bowl; cover with boiling water. Stand 2 minutes; drain. Rinse under cold water; drain. Cut asparagus and onions to same width as beef.

2 Lay beef slices flat; sift 1 tablespoon of the cornflour lightly over top. Lay two pieces each of carrot and onion, and one piece of asparagus across dusted side of each slice of beef; roll up. Tie rolls with string or secure ends with toothpicks. Dust rolls lightly with remaining cornflour.

3 Heat oil in medium frying pan. Cook rolls until browned lightly all over; remove rolls from pan. Wipe oil from pan with absorbent paper; return rolls to pan. Add combined sugar, mirin, sake and sauce; bring to a boil. Reduce heat; simmer, turning occasionally, until rolls are cooked through. If a thicker sauce is preferred, remove rolls and boil sauce to reduce. Return rolls to pan and coat with sauce.

4 Remove rolls from pan; cool 2 minutes. Remove and discard toothpicks; cut rolls in half. Arrange on serving plate with snow pea sprouts; serve with remaining sauce.

serves 4

per serving 10.8g fat; 1283kJ

tips Vegetables can be used raw as they will cook in the rolls, but they should be cut more thinly. Very thinly sliced beef, sold as yakiniku or sukiyaki beef, is available from Asian grocery stores. To make larger rolls, use two slices of meat, slightly overlapping. Pork fillet or rib eye steak (scotch fillet) can be substituted for eye fillet, if preferred.

deep-fried tofu
in broth

PREPARATION TIME 15 MINUTES (plus standing time) ▥ COOKING TIME 15 MINUTES

300g firm tofu
2 tablespoons cornflour
vegetable oil, for deep-frying
3/4 cup (180ml) dashi stock
2 tablespoons japanese soy sauce
2 tablespoons mirin
2 tablespoons finely grated daikon
1 tablespoon grated fresh ginger
1 green onion, chopped finely
2 teaspoons smoked dried bonito flakes (katsuobushi)

1 Press tofu between two chopping boards with a weight on top.
Raise one end; stand 25 minutes.

2 Cut tofu into eight even-sized pieces; pat dry between layers of
absorbent paper. Toss in cornflour; shake away excess cornflour.
Heat oil in medium saucepan or deep-fryer; cook tofu, in batches, until
browned lightly all over. Drain on absorbent paper.

3 Combine dashi, sauce and mirin in small saucepan; bring to a boil.

4 Place two pieces of tofu in each serving bowl; divide daikon, ginger
and onion among bowls. Pour over equal amounts of dashi mixture;
top with bonito flakes.

serves 4

per serving 9.9g fat; 688kJ
tip Instead of serving tofu with accompaniments, try seasoning the cornflour with
chilli flakes, sesame seeds or seven-spice mix (sichimi togarashi).

crumbed
pork fillets

PREPARATION TIME 15 MINUTES (plus standing time) ■ COOKING TIME 15 MINUTES

2 pork steaks (600g)

¼ cup (35g) plain flour

2 eggs, beaten lightly

2 teaspoons water

**2 cups (100g) dried
  japanese breadcrumbs**

**6 cups finely shredded
  cabbage (300g)**

vegetable oil, for deep-frying

1 lemon, cut into wedges

3 teaspoons japanese mustard

tonkatsu sauce

**2 tablespoons japanese
  worcestershire sauce**

⅓ cup (80ml) tomato sauce

1 teaspoon japanese soy sauce

2 tablespoons sake

1 teaspoon japanese mustard

1 Using meat mallet, pound pork gently. Toss in flour, shaking off excess.

2 Dip pork in combined egg and water; coat in breadcrumbs.

3 Soak cabbage in iced water 5 minutes to crisp; drain.

4 Heat enough oil to cover pork in medium saucepan or deep-fryer. Cook pork, in batches, turning occasionally, 5 minutes or until golden brown on both sides. Skim oil during cooking to remove any breadcrumbs.

5 Drain pork on absorbent paper; cut diagonally into 2cm slices. Place cabbage on serving plate; arrange pork on top so it appears uncut. Serve with lemon wedges, mustard to taste and tonkatsu sauce.

tonkatsu sauce Combine ingredients in small saucepan. Bring to a boil; whisk. Remove from heat; cool.

serves 4

per serving 17g fat; 1873kJ

tips Tonkatsu, a rich, fruity barbecue sauce, is especially suited to this dish and is also available ready-made from Asian grocery stores. Japanese breadcrumbs are very light and crunchy. They are available in two crumb sizes; both are suitable.

sweet soy
pumpkin

PREPARATION TIME 10 MINUTES ■ COOKING TIME 15 MINUTES

500g pumpkin, unpeeled
1½ cups (375ml) dashi stock
1½ tablespoons sugar
2 tablespoons mirin
1 tablespoon japanese soy sauce

1 Cut pumpkin into 5cm pieces; discard seeds. Slice skin off at random to give surface a mottled appearance and to allow flavour of broth to be absorbed.

2 Place pumpkin in medium saucepan, skin side down; add dashi, sugar and mirin. Bring to a boil; reduce heat. Simmer, covered, 5 minutes, turning pumpkin after 2 minutes.

3 Add sauce; cook 8 minutes or until pumpkin is tender, turning pieces halfway through cooking time. Do not allow pumpkin to overcook or it will fall apart. Remove from heat; allow to cool in liquid a few minutes before dividing among individual serving bowls. Serve hot or at room temperature, drizzled with some of the liquid.

serves 4

per serving 0.5g fat; 327kJ
tip Add stir-fried minced pork or chicken to pumpkin for a more substantial dish.

prawn, cucumber and
wakame salad

PREPARATION TIME 20 MINUTES (plus standing and marinating time) ■ COOKING TIME 2 MINUTES

1 lebanese cucumber (130g)

1/2 teaspoon salt

4 medium cooked prawns (100g)

10g dried seaweed (wakame)

**2cm piece fresh ginger (20g),
  sliced thinly**

dressing

1/4 cup (60ml) rice vinegar

1 1/2 tablespoons dashi stock

1 1/2 tablespoons japanese soy sauce

3 teaspoons sugar

1 1/2 tablespoons mirin

1 Halve cucumber lengthways. Using spoon, scrape out seeds; slice thinly.

2 Place cucumber in small bowl. Sprinkle with salt; stand 15 minutes. Transfer to colander or sieve; rinse under cold running water. Drain; pat dry with absorbent paper. Shell and devein prawns; halve lengthways. Place in medium bowl with 1 tablespoon of the dressing; stand 10 minutes. Add cucumber.

3 Meanwhile, place seaweed in small bowl; cover with cold water. Stand 5 minutes or until seaweed softens; drain. Add seaweed to bowl with cucumber, prawns, ginger and remaining dressing; mix gently. Divide among individual serving bowls.

dressing Combine ingredients in small saucepan; bring to a boil. Reduce heat; simmer, stirring until sugar dissolves. Remove from heat; cool.

serves 4

per serving 0.2g fat; 171kJ

tips Cooked crab meat can be substituted for the prawns, if preferred.

Wakame is a highly nutritious seaweed which is dark when dry, but reconstitutes to a bright green colour. The leaves are usually stripped from the central vein.

vietnam

Vietnamese food is characterised by fresh sharp flavours.
The heat of chilli and the pungency of fish sauce are countered by the
liberal use of fresh lemon grass, coriander, vietnamese mint and lime.
It's a deliciously light cuisine, making the
most of an abundant supply of
fresh vegetables and herbs.

chicken noodle soup

PREPARATION TIME 25 MINUTES ■ COOKING TIME 40 MINUTES

2 chicken breast fillets (340g)

30g chicken livers, sliced thinly

2 litres (8 cups) water

1 teaspoon grated fresh ginger

3 cloves garlic

2 x 12cm stems fresh lemon grass, bruised

1 medium brown onion (150g), sliced thickly

¼ teaspoon black peppercorns

8 dried shiitake mushrooms

2 tablespoons fish sauce

50g bean thread noodles

3 green onions, chopped finely

¼ cup coarsely chopped fresh coriander

160g bean sprouts, tips trimmed

1 Separate tenderloin section from each chicken fillet. Place fillets between pieces of plastic; using meat mallet, gently pound fillets to an even thickness.

2 Place livers, the water, ginger, garlic, lemon grass, brown onion and peppercorns in large saucepan; stir over heat until mixture boils. Add chicken; reduce heat. Simmer, uncovered, about 5 minutes or until chicken is just tender; skim stock. Remove chicken from stock; slice thinly. Continue to simmer stock, uncovered, about 30 minutes or until reduced to about 1.5 litres (6 cups). Strain stock; discard liver mixture. Return stock to cleaned pan.

3 Meanwhile, place mushrooms in medium heatproof bowl. Cover with boiling water; stand 20 minutes. Drain mushrooms; reserve ⅓ cup (80ml) of the liquid. Discard stems; slice caps thinly. Add reserved mushroom liquid, sauce and noodles to stock in pan; simmer, uncovered, a few minutes or until noodles are soft. Stir in mushrooms, chicken and green onion. Just before serving, stir in coriander and sprouts.

serves 4

per serving 9.1g fat; 1010kJ

gingered prawn rolls

PREPARATION TIME 20 MINUTES (plus marinating time) ■ COOKING TIME 5 MINUTES

1.5kg medium uncooked prawns

¼ cup (100g) grated fresh ginger

3 cloves garlic, crushed

2 tablespoons finely grated kaffir lime rind

¼ cup (65g) finely chopped palm sugar

⅓ cup (80ml) sweet chilli sauce

⅓ cup (80ml) chicken stock

12 sheets rice paper

48 baby spinach leaves (50g)

½ cup (125ml) light soy sauce

1 Shell and devein prawns; chop coarsely. Combine prawns, ginger, garlic, rind and sugar in large bowl. Cover; refrigerate at least 3 hours or until required. *[Can be made a day ahead to this stage.]*

2 Heat oiled large frying pan. Cook prawn mixture, in batches, until prawns just change colour; transfer to large heatproof bowl. Place chilli sauce and stock in pan; simmer, stirring, until sauce boils and thickens. Pour over prawns.

3 Place one sheet of rice paper in medium bowl of warm water until just softened; carefully lift from water and place on board. Place four spinach leaves on centre of rice paper; top with 2 heaped tablespoons prawn mixture. Fold in top and bottom; roll from side to enclose filling. Repeat with remaining rice paper, spinach and prawn mixture. Serve with soy sauce and lime wedges, if desired.

serves 4

per roll 1.9g fat; 1160kJ

tip Can be made 3 hours ahead and refrigerated, covered.

pho bo

PREPARATION TIME 30 MINUTES ■ COOKING TIME 2 HOURS 30 MINUTES

1.5kg beef bones

**2 medium brown onions (300g),
chopped coarsely**

**2 medium carrots (240g),
chopped coarsely**

**4 trimmed sticks celery (300g),
chopped coarsely**

2 cinnamon sticks

4 star anise

6 cardamom pods, bruised

10 black peppercorns

2 tablespoons fish sauce

6 cloves

60g piece fresh ginger, sliced thinly

6 cloves garlic, sliced thinly

500g piece gravy beef

4 litres (16 cups) water

2 tablespoons soy sauce

200g bean thread noodles

100g bean sprouts

**1/2 cup loosely packed fresh
vietnamese mint**

4 fresh red thai chillies, sliced thinly

**1 medium brown onion (150g),
sliced thinly, extra**

**1/2 cup loosely packed
fresh coriander**

1 Preheat oven to hot. Combine beef bones, onion, carrot and celery in large baking dish; roast in hot oven, uncovered, about 45 minutes or until browned all over. Drain excess fat from dish.

2 Combine beef mixture, cinnamon, star anise, cardamom, peppercorns, fish sauce, cloves, ginger, garlic, gravy beef and the water in large saucepan; bring to a boil. Reduce heat; simmer, uncovered, 1 1/2 hours, skimming occasionally. Strain through muslin-lined strainer into large bowl. Reserve broth and beef; discard bones and spices. When beef is cool enough to handle, shred finely; return with soy sauce and broth to cleaned pan. *[Can be made a day ahead to this stage and refrigerated, covered, or frozen for up to 3 months.]*

3 Just before serving, place noodles in large heatproof bowl; cover with boiling water. Stand 3 minutes; drain. Add vermicelli to pan; stir over heat until hot. Serve with sprouts, mint, chilli, extra onion and coriander.

serves 6

per serving 5.3g fat; 1000kJ

tips Accompany with more raw greens, such as basil leaves, regular garden mint leaves or finely shredded cabbage.

Chicken is often substituted for beef in pho recipes.

Try adding various kinds of offal, such as tripe, as the Vietnamese do.

spicy fried
noodles

PREPARATION TIME 15 MINUTES (plus standing time) ■ COOKING TIME 15 MINUTES

200g thick rice stick noodles

500g medium uncooked prawns

2 teaspoons peanut oil

150g pork fillet, sliced thinly

4 cloves garlic, crushed

2 teaspoons grated fresh ginger

¼ cup (60ml) lime juice

¼ cup (60ml) fish sauce

2 teaspoons sugar

80g bean sprouts, tips trimmed

⅓ cup (45g) unsalted roasted peanuts, chopped coarsely

¼ cup coarsely chopped fresh coriander

4 green onions, chopped coarsely

1 medium carrot (120g), grated coarsely

1 Place noodles in large heatproof bowl; cover with boiling water. Stand until just soft; drain. Shell and devein prawns.

2 Heat oil in large wok or frying pan; stir-fry pork and prawns until tender.

3 Add garlic, ginger, juice, sauce and sugar to pork mixture; simmer, uncovered, 2 minutes.

4 Add remaining ingredients and noodles; stir-fry until mixture is heated through.

serves 4

per serving 9.5g fat; 1409kJ

clay pot
chicken

PREPARATION TIME 15 MINUTES (plus marinating time) ■ COOKING TIME 1 HOUR

1kg chicken thigh fillets, halved

2 small brown onions (160g), quartered

340g baby bok choy, chopped coarsely

½ cup (125ml) chicken stock

marinade

4 cloves garlic, crushed

1 tablespoon fish sauce

1 tablespoon soy sauce

1 tablespoon hoisin sauce

2 tablespoons lime juice

2 tablespoons finely chopped fresh lemon grass

1 Combine chicken and marinade in large bowl; mix well. Cover; refrigerate 3 hours or until required. *[Can be made a day ahead to this stage or frozen for up to a month.]*

2 Place chicken mixture with remaining ingredients in clay pot or 2.5-litre (10 cup) ovenproof dish; mix gently. Bake, covered, in moderate oven about 1 hour or until chicken is tender.

marinade Combine ingredients in small bowl; mix well.

serves 6

per serving 12.5g fat; 1087kJ

tips Recipe can be made a day ahead and refrigerated, covered; serve with hokkien noodles, if desired.

We used a clay pot from an Asian food store and soaked it in cold water overnight before using.

spicy fried squid
with onions

PREPARATION TIME 10 MINUTES (plus marinating time) ▓ COOKING TIME 15 MINUTES

1kg squid hoods
3 teaspoons salt
1 tablespoon sugar
1/2 teaspoon chilli powder
1/4 teaspoon ground ginger
1 clove garlic, crushed
1 cup (150g) plain flour
2 teaspoons ground black pepper
vegetable oil, for deep-frying

onion rings
3 medium white onions (450g), sliced thickly
plain flour

1 Cut squid hoods along one side and open out. Score inside of hoods using sharp knife in a diagonal pattern, without cutting all the way through. Cut into 3cm x 5cm pieces.

2 Combine squid, salt, sugar, chilli powder, ginger and garlic in large bowl; mix well. Cover; refrigerate 3 hours or until required. *[Can be made a day ahead to this stage.]*

3 Toss squid in combined flour and pepper; shake off excess flour mixture.

4 Heat oil in heated large wok or frying pan; deep-fry squid, in batches, until tender (this takes only a minute or two). Drain on absorbent paper. Serve squid with onion rings and thinly sliced green onions, if desired.

onion rings Toss onion rings in flour; shake off excess flour. Deep-fry onion rings in batches in hot oil until browned; drain on absorbent paper.

serves 6

per serving 16.8g fat; 1647kJ

stuffed chicken wings

PREPARATION TIME 40 MINUTES (plus standing and cooling time) ■ COOKING TIME 30 MINUTES

25g bean thread noodles

1 dried wood ear fungus

2 teaspoons peanut oil

1 green onion, chopped finely

2 tablespoons finely chopped fresh lemon grass

4 cloves garlic, crushed

1 tablespoon fish sauce

100g minced pork

1 small carrot (70g), grated finely

10 drained canned water chestnuts (30g), chopped finely

2 tablespoons finely chopped fresh coriander

250g medium uncooked prawns, shelled, deveined, chopped finely

12 large chicken wings (1.5kg)

vegetable oil, for deep-frying

1 Place noodles in large heatproof bowl. Cover with boiling water; stand until tender. Drain noodles; chop into 2cm lengths. Place fungus in small heatproof bowl; cover with boiling water. Stand 20 minutes; drain. Discard stem; chop finely.

2 Heat peanut oil in heated large wok or frying pan; stir-fry onion, lemon grass, garlic, sauce, pork, carrot, chestnuts, coriander and fungus about 3 minutes or until pork is cooked. Add prawns; stir over heat until prawns change colour. Stir in noodles; cool.

3 Cut thick section from chicken wings, leaving the middle piece and wing tip intact. (Use thick sections for another dish.)

4 Twist one wing at the middle joint to break the joint. Holding bone, scrape meat away from bone without piercing skin; pull out and discard bone. Repeat with remaining wings.

5 Three-quarter fill cavities with pork mixture (this allows for skin to shrink); secure openings with toothpicks. *[Can be made a day ahead to this stage and refrigerated, covered.]*

6 Heat vegetable oil in heated large wok or frying pan. Deep-fry wings, in batches, until browned lightly and cooked through; drain on absorbent paper. Serve on snow pea sprouts, if desired.

makes 12

per wing 22.4g fat; 1215kJ

rice paper rolls

PREPARATION TIME 20 MINUTES (plus refrigeration time) ■ COOKING TIME 10 MINUTES

80g bean thread noodles

1 tablespoon peanut oil

600g chicken breast fillets

⅓ cup (80ml) peanut oil, extra

1 tablespoon sesame oil

⅓ cup (80ml) mirin

2 tablespoons finely chopped fresh lemon grass

2 teaspoons fish sauce

2 teaspoons ketjap manis

1 tablespoon finely chopped fresh ginger

2 cloves garlic, crushed

½ cup shredded fresh mint

1 small red onion (100g), sliced thinly

½ cup (70g) cashews, toasted, chopped finely

80g bean sprouts, tips trimmed

2 tablespoons grated lime rind

4 fresh red thai chillies, seeded, chopped finely

16 round rice paper sheets

16 fresh mint leaves, extra

½ cup (125ml) mirin, extra

¼ cup (60ml) ketjap manis, extra

⅓ cup (80ml) lime juice

1 Place noodles in small heatproof bowl; cover with boiling water. Stand until just tender; drain. Cut noodles into 4cm lengths.

2 Heat peanut oil in medium saucepan; cook chicken until tender and browned on both sides. Cut chicken into thin slices.

3 Combine extra peanut oil, sesame oil, mirin, lemon grass, sauce, ketjap manis, ginger, garlic and mint in large bowl; stir in noodles, chicken, onion, cashews, sprouts, rind and chilli. Cover; refrigerate 30 minutes. *[Can be made 3 hours ahead to this stage.]*

4 Place one sheet of rice paper in medium bowl of warm water until just softened; carefully lift from water and place on board. Place one mint leaf in centre of rice paper; top with 1 heaped tablespoon of the filling. Roll to enclose, folding in ends. Repeat with remaining rice paper sheets, mint and filling.

5 Combine extra mirin, extra ketjap manis and juice in small bowl; serve as a dipping sauce with rolls.

makes 16

per roll 12.1g fat; 823kJ

tip Rice paper rolls and sauce can be made 3 hours ahead and refrigerated, covered.

twice-cooked
duck

PREPARATION TIME 15 MINUTES (plus cooling and marinating time)
COOKING TIME 2 HOURS

1.7kg duck
1 tablespoon peanut oil
2 cloves garlic, crushed
1 tablespoon grated fresh ginger
2 tablespoons sweet chilli sauce
1/4 teaspoon five-spice powder

ginger sauce
3 cups (750ml) chicken stock
1 large orange (300g), peeled
50g piece fresh ginger, sliced thinly
2 tablespoons brown sugar
2 green onions, chopped finely
2 teaspoons cornflour
1/4 cup (60ml) water

1 Place duck in baking dish. Bake, uncovered, in moderate oven about 1 hour or until tender; cool. Cut duck in half lengthways; remove and discard rib and back bones.

2 Combine oil, garlic, ginger, sauce and five-spice in small bowl; mix well. Place duck in shallow dish; brush chilli mixture over duck. Cover; refrigerate 3 hours or until required. *[Can be made a day ahead to this stage.]*

3 Place duck, skin-side up, on wire rack over baking dish. Bake, uncovered, in moderately hot oven about 45 minutes or until skin is crisp. Pour ginger sauce over duck; serve with bean sprouts, baby spinach, green onion and coriander, if desired.

ginger sauce Place stock, whole orange and ginger in medium saucepan; simmer, uncovered, about 30 minutes or until reduced to about 1 1/2 cups (375ml). Strain; return strained sauce to pan. Add sugar, onion and blended cornflour and water; stir over heat until mixture boils and thickens slightly. *[Can be made a day ahead and refrigerated, covered.]*

serves 4

per serving 95g fat; 4316kJ

barbecued pork
with crisp noodles

PREPARATION TIME 30 MINUTES (plus marinating time) ■ COOKING TIME 25 MINUTES

500g pork fillets

3 green onions, chopped finely

3 cloves garlic, crushed

2 teaspoons sugar

2 tablespoons fish sauce

¼ cup (60ml) lime juice

¼ teaspoon cracked black pepper

2 teaspoons grated fresh ginger

**¼ cup finely chopped
  fresh coriander**

**2 fresh red thai chillies,
  chopped finely**

vegetable oil, for deep-frying

100g thick rice stick noodles

**3 medium brown onions (450g),
  sliced thinly**

½ cup (125ml) water

1 Combine pork, green onion, garlic, sugar, sauce, juice, pepper, ginger, coriander and chilli in large bowl; mix well. Cover, refrigerate several hours or until required. *[Can be made a day ahead to this stage.]*

2 Remove pork from marinade; reserve marinade. Cook pork on heated, oiled grill plate (or grill or barbecue), turning occasionally, until browned all over and cooked as desired; wrap in foil.

3 Heat oil in heated large wok or frying pan. Deep-fry noodles, in batches, until puffed; drain on absorbent paper.

4 Deep-fry brown onion, in batches, in hot oil until browned; drain on absorbent paper.

5 Add reserved marinade and the water to medium saucepan; simmer, uncovered, about 5 minutes or until reduced to about ½ cup (125ml). Slice pork thinly. Gently combine with noodles and onions in large bowl; drizzle with marinade mixture.

serves 4

per serving 11.5g fat; 1421kJ

stir-fried
mixed vegetables

PREPARATION TIME 15 MINUTES (plus standing time) ■ COOKING TIME 10 MINUTES

190g fried bean curd, cut into
  1cm slices

1/3 cup (80ml) soy sauce

2 tablespoons coarsely chopped
  fresh coriander

1 teaspoon honey

6 dried shiitake mushrooms

1 tablespoon peanut oil

3 cloves garlic, crushed

1 1/2 teaspoons grated fresh ginger

1 tablespoon finely chopped fresh
  lemon grass

2 medium carrots (240g), cut into
  6cm strips

200g snake beans, cut into
  6cm lengths

500g cauliflower, cut into florets

230g canned bamboo shoots,
  rinsed, drained

600g chinese cabbage,
  chopped coarsely

3/4 cup (180ml) vegetable stock

1 tablespoon cornflour

2 teaspoons hoisin sauce

1 teaspoon lime juice

1/2 teaspoon sambal oelek

1 Combine bean curd, soy sauce, coriander and honey in small bowl.

2 Place mushrooms in medium heatproof bowl; cover with boiling water. Stand 20 minutes; drain. Discard stems; slice caps.

3 Heat oil in heated large wok or frying pan; stir-fry garlic, ginger and lemon grass until fragrant. Add carrots, beans and cauliflower; stir-fry until vegetables are just tender.

4 Add bean curd mixture to wok with bamboo shoots, mushrooms and cabbage; stir-fry until heated through. Stir in blended stock, cornflour, sauce, juice and sambal oelek; stir over heat until mixture boils and thickens slightly.

serves 6

per serving 7.2g fat; 637kJ

coconut
pork and prawns

PREPARATION TIME 20 MINUTES ■ COOKING TIME 1 HOUR 10 MINUTES

1½ tablespoons peanut oil
2 teaspoons grated fresh ginger
2 cloves garlic, crushed
½ teaspoon ground turmeric
1 fresh red thai chilli, chopped finely
2 tablespoons finely chopped fresh lemon grass
1 medium brown onion (150g), sliced thinly
500g diced pork
1²/₃ cups (410ml) coconut cream
1 tablespoon fish sauce
1 teaspoon grated lime rind
230g can bamboo shoots, drained
½ cup (75g) unsalted roasted peanuts, chopped coarsely
500g medium uncooked prawns, shelled, deveined
¼ cup finely chopped fresh basil
¼ cup finely chopped fresh mint

1 Heat 1 tablespoon of the oil in heated large wok or frying pan. Cook ginger, garlic, turmeric, chilli, lemon grass and onion; stir until onion is soft. Remove from wok.

2 Heat remaining oil in wok. Cook pork; stir until browned all over.

3 Return onion mixture to wok with coconut cream, sauce, rind, bamboo shoots and nuts; mix well.

4 Cover wok; simmer about 1 hour or until pork is tender. Stir in prawns and herbs; simmer, uncovered, a few minutes or until prawns are tender.

serves 4

per serving 39.8g fat; 2434kJ

herbed
chicken salad

PREPARATION TIME 45 MINUTES ■ COOKING TIME 15 MINUTES

500g chicken breast fillets

¼ cup (60ml) peanut oil

¼ cup (60ml) rice vinegar

2 teaspoons fish sauce

1 teaspoon finely grated lime rind

¼ cup (60ml) lime juice

2 fresh red thai chillies, seeded, chopped finely

2 cloves garlic, crushed

2 tablespoons brown sugar

½ cup firmly packed, coarsely shredded fresh vietnamese mint

½ cup firmly packed, coarsely shredded fresh coriander

500g finely shredded chinese cabbage

2 medium carrots (240g), grated coarsely

6 green onions, sliced thinly

⅓ cup (35g) coarsely chopped unsalted roasted peanuts

1 Poach chicken in medium frying pan containing 1 litre (4 cups) boiling water. As soon as water returns to a boil, turn heat to low; simmer gently, uncovered, about 15 minutes or until chicken is cooked through.

2 Pour chicken into large strainer over large heatproof bowl; reserve poaching liquid for another use. When cool enough to handle, slice chicken thinly.

3 Combine oil, vinegar, sauce, rind and juice in large bowl with chilli, garlic and sugar; stir until sugar completely dissolves. Add mint and two-thirds of the coriander; toss gently to combine.

4 Add chicken, cabbage and carrot to the dressing mixture; toss gently to combine. Divide salad among serving bowls; sprinkle with equal amounts of remaining coriander, onion and nuts.

serves 4

per serving 23.3g fat; 1968k

lemon grass
chicken

PREPARATION TIME 20 MINUTES (plus marinating and standing time) ■ COOKING TIME 20 MINUTES

**700g chicken breast fillets,
sliced thickly**

**¼ cup finely chopped fresh
lemon grass**

1 tablespoon grated fresh ginger

4 kaffir lime leaves, shredded

4 baby eggplants (240g)

coarse cooking salt

¼ cup (60ml) peanut oil

**1 medium white onion (150g),
sliced thinly**

2 teaspoons ground cumin

500g asparagus, cut into 5cm lengths

**1 tablespoon finely grated
lemon rind**

1 teaspoon lemon juice

1 Combine chicken, lemon grass, ginger and lime leaves in large bowl. Cover; refrigerate 3 hours or until required. *[Can be made a day ahead to this stage or frozen for up to a month.]*

2 Halve eggplants lengthways; cut halves into 2cm pieces. Place eggplant in colander. Sprinkle all over with salt; stand 30 minutes. Rinse eggplant under cold running water; pat dry with absorbent paper.

3 Heat 1 tablespoon of the oil in heated large wok or frying pan; stir-fry chicken mixture and onion, in batches, until chicken is browned and cooked through.

4 Heat remaining oil in wok; stir-fry eggplant with cumin until tender.

5 Return chicken mixture to wok. Add asparagus, rind and juice; stir-fry, tossing to combine with eggplant mixture. Serve topped with sliced fresh red chilli, if desired.

serves 4

per serving 23.7g fat; 1669kJ

fish
with sweet chilli sauce

PREPARATION TIME 15 MINUTES ■ COOKING TIME 15 MINUTES

1 cup (150g) plain flour
1/3 cup (50g) cornflour
1 teaspoon sugar
1/4 teaspoon ground turmeric
2 green onions, chopped finely
2 egg whites
3/4 cup (180ml) water
vegetable oil, for deep-frying
12 small boneless white fish fillets (900g)

sweet chilli sauce
2 tablespoons soy sauce
2/3 cup (160ml) sweet chilli sauce
2 tablespoons brown malt vinegar
1 tablespoon brown sugar
1/2 cup (125ml) chicken stock
2 tablespoons finely chopped fresh coriander
2 teaspoons cornflour
1/4 cup (60ml) water

1 Sift flours, sugar and turmeric into large bowl; stir in onion and combined egg whites and water. Mix to a smooth batter.

2 Heat oil in heated large wok or frying pan. Dip fish fillets, separately, in batter to coat completely; drain off excess batter. Deep-fry fish, in batches, until browned lightly and cooked through; drain on absorbent paper. Serve with sweet chilli sauce.

sweet chilli sauce Combine sauces, vinegar, sugar, stock and coriander in small saucepan. Stir in blended cornflour and water; stir over heat until mixture boils and thickens slightly. *[Can be made 3 days ahead and refrigerated, covered.]*

serves 4

per serving 24g fat; 2678kJ

lemon grass and asparagus
beef

PREPARATION TIME 15 MINUTES (plus standing time) ■ COOKING TIME 15 MINUTES

500g piece beef fillet, sliced thinly

3 cloves garlic, crushed

2 tablespoons finely chopped fresh lemon grass

1 teaspoon sugar

1 teaspoon salt

2 tablespoons peanut oil

1 large white onion (200g)

2 medium tomatoes (360g)

250g asparagus, halved

1 teaspoon grated fresh ginger

2 teaspoons fresh coriander

2 tablespoons unsalted roasted peanuts

1 Combine beef, garlic, lemon grass, sugar, salt and half of the oil in large bowl. Cover; refrigerate 3 hours or until required. *[Can be made 2 days ahead to this stage or frozen for up to 3 months.]*

2 Cut onion and tomatoes into wedges. Boil, steam or microwave asparagus until just tender. Rinse under cold running water; drain. Heat remaining oil in heated large wok or frying pan. Stir-fry onion and ginger until onion is soft; remove from wok. Stir-fry beef, in batches, until browned.

3 Return beef to wok. Add onion mixture, tomato and asparagus; stir-fry until heated through. Serve sprinkled with coriander and peanuts.

serves 4

per serving 17.9g fat; 1308kJ

stir-fried squid
with pickled mustard cabbage

PREPARATION TIME 25 MINUTES (plus marinating time) ■ COOKING TIME 20 MINUTES

600g squid hoods

4 cloves garlic, crushed

2 tablespoons lime juice

1 tablespoon fish sauce

1 tablespoon oyster sauce

1 tablespoon soy sauce

2 tablespoons peanut oil

2 large tomatoes (500g)

1 medium brown onion (150g), quartered

1 medium red capsicum (200g), sliced thickly

4 green onions, chopped finely

350g pickled mustard cabbage rinsed, drained, sliced thickly

2 fresh red thai chillies, seeded, sliced thinly

1 Cut squid hoods along one side and open out. Score inside of hoods with a sharp knife in a diagonal pattern, without cutting all the way through. Cut into 4cm pieces.

2 Combine garlic, juice, sauces and squid in large bowl. Cover; refrigerate 1 hour or until required. *[Can be made a day ahead to this stage.]*

3 Drain squid; reserve marinade.

4 Heat half of the oil in heated large wok or frying pan. Stir-fry squid, in batches, over high heat until just tender; remove from wok. Cut tomatoes into wedges. Heat remaining oil in wok; stir-fry tomato and vegetables over medium heat until onion is soft. Add squid, reserved marinade, mustard cabbage and chilli; stir over heat until mixture boils.

serves 4

per serving 11.8g fat, 1338kJ

beef
and rice noodle salad

PREPARATION TIME 10 MINUTES ■ COOKING TIME 10 MINUTES

400g beef rump steak
100g thin rice stick noodles
150g snow peas
1 telegraph cucumber (400g)
1 tablespoon fresh coriander

lime and chilli dressing
¼ cup (60ml) lime juice
2 tablespoons peanut oil
1 fresh red thai chilli, seeded, sliced thinly

1 Cook beef on heated oiled grill plate (or grill or barbecue) until browned on both sides and cooked as desired; cover. Rest 5 minutes; slice thinly.

2 Meanwhile, cook noodles in large saucepan of boiling water, uncovered, about 2 minutes or until just tender; drain. Rinse under cold running water; drain.

3 Cut snow peas in half diagonally. Cut cucumber in half lengthways. Remove seeds; slice diagonally.

4 Gently toss beef, noodles, snow peas and cucumber in large bowl with dressing; sprinkle with coriander.

lime and chilli dressing Combine ingredients in screw-top jar; shake well. *[Can be made 2 days ahead and refrigerated, covered.]*

serves 4

per serving 16.6g fat; 1333kJ

stir-fry beef
and noodle

PREPARATION TIME 10 MINUTES (plus marinating time) ■ COOKING TIME 15 MINUTES

750g piece beef rump, sliced thinly

1/4 cup (60ml) fish sauce

1/3 cup (80ml) oyster sauce

1/3 cup (80ml) sweet chilli sauce

3 cloves garlic, crushed

500g hokkien noodles

2 tablespoons peanut oil

2 large brown onions (400g), sliced thinly

200g snow peas

80g bean sprouts, tips trimmed

1 Place beef in large bowl with half of the combined sauces and garlic. Cover; refrigerate 3 hours or until required. *[Can be made 2 days ahead to this stage or frozen for up to 3 months.]*

2 Rinse noodles under hot running water; drain. Transfer to large bowl; separate with fork.

3 Heat half of the oil in heated large wok or frying pan. Stir-fry beef mixture, in batches, until browned all over and almost cooked; remove from wok.

4 Heat remaining oil in wok; stir-fry onion until soft. Add snow peas and sprouts; stir-fry 1 minute. Return beef and noodles to wok with remaining combined sauces and garlic; stir-fry until hot.

serves 4

per serving 20.2g fat; 3155kJ

spiced
caramel pork

PREPARATION TIME 10 MINUTES ■ COOKING TIME 35 MINUTES

1 large white onion (300g)
1 tablespoon peanut oil
750g pork neck, cut into 3cm pieces
1 cup (250ml) water
1/3 cup (75g) sugar
1 tablespoon fish sauce
1/2 teaspoon sambal oelek
1/4 teaspoon five-spice powder
1 green onion, chopped finely

1 Cut onion into wedges. Heat oil in large frying pan; cook pork, stirring, until browned and tender. Add onion; cook, stirring, until onion is soft. Cover pan; remove from heat.

2 Combine 1/4 cup (60ml) of the water with sugar in small saucepan; stir over heat, without boiling, until sugar dissolves. Boil, uncovered, without stirring, until sugar syrup is golden brown. Add the remaining water and fish sauce to sugar syrup; stir over low heat until smooth. Reduce heat; simmer, uncovered, until reduced to about 1/2 cup (125ml).

3 Stir sauce mixture into pork in pan with sambal oelek and spice; simmer, uncovered, about 5 minutes or until pork is heated through. Serve sprinkled with green onion. Serve with steamed rice, if desired.

serves 4

per serving 11.8g fat; 1526kJ

crunchy vegetables
with noodles

PREPARATION TIME 20 MINUTES (plus standing time) ■ COOKING TIME 10 MINUTES

2 eggs, beaten lightly

1 teaspoon water

2 teaspoons peanut oil

50g bean thread noodles

5 dried shiitake mushrooms

1 medium carrot (120g)

150g snow peas, sliced thinly

**1/2 cup (60g) drained canned
bamboo shoots, sliced thinly**

**1 lebanese cucumber (130g),
peeled, seeded, sliced thinly**

**1 medium red capsicum (200g),
sliced thinly**

**1 small green capsicum (150g),
sliced thinly**

**1 small brown onion (80g),
sliced thinly**

**230g can water chestnuts,
drained, sliced thinly**

**1/4 cup coarsely chopped
fresh coriander**

**2 teaspoons white sesame
seeds, toasted**

dressing

3 cloves garlic, crushed

2 teaspoons sugar

1/4 cup (60ml) lime juice

1 tablespoon sesame oil

2 teaspoons fish sauce

1 tablespoon soy sauce

2 tablespoons rice vinegar

1 tablespoon hoisin sauce

1 Combine eggs and the water in small bowl. Heat half of the oil in
24cm omelette pan; pour in half of the egg mixture. Tilt pan to cover base
with egg mixture; cook until omelette is set. Remove; cool. Repeat with
remaining oil and egg mixture. Roll omelettes tightly; slice thickly.

2 Place noodles in large heatproof bowl; cover with boiling water. Stand until
just soft; drain. Place mushrooms in medium heatproof bowl; cover with
boiling water. Stand 20 minutes; drain. Discard stems; slice caps thinly.

3 Using vegetable peeler, peel long, thin strips from carrot.

4 Combine carrot with remaining vegetables, noodles, mushrooms,
water chestnuts and coriander in large bowl. Add dressing; mix well. Top
with omelette and sesame seeds.

dressing Combine ingredients in screw-top jar; shake well.

serves 6

per serving 8.9g fat; 696kJ
tip Recipe can be made 3 hours ahead and refrigerated, covered.

mango coconut whiz

PREPARATION TIME 10 MINUTES

½ cup (125ml) water
1 cup (250ml) pureed mango
1²/₃ cups (410ml) coconut cream
2 teaspoons sugar
2 tablespoons lime juice
12 ice cubes
2 tablespoons flaked coconut, toasted

1 Blend or process the water, mango, coconut cream, sugar, juice and ice cubes until smooth. Pour into glasses; sprinkle with coconut.

makes 4 cups

per cup 22.8g fat; 1128kJ
tip You will need about 3 small mangoes for this recipe.

lychee sunrise cocktail

PREPARATION TIME 5 MINUTES

2 cups (500ml) orange juice
grenadine syrup
500g fresh lychees
1½ teaspoons sugar
⅓ cup (80ml) gin
12 ice cubes
1 tablespoon lime juice

1 Divide orange juice evenly among four large glasses. Add a few drops of grenadine to each glass; stir once to give a marbled effect.

2 Blend or process remaining ingredients until smooth. Carefully pour lychee mixture over orange juice mixture in each glass.

makes 4 cups

per cup 0.5g fat; 810kJ

mixed fruit lassi

PREPARATION TIME 15 MINUTES

- ½ small pawpaw (400g)
- 1 large orange (300g)
- 2 medium kiwi fruit (170g)
- ½ small pineapple (400g)
- 75g blueberries
- 150g raspberries
- ¼ cup (60ml) fresh passionfruit pulp
- ½ cup (125ml) yogurt

1 Peel pawpaw, orange, kiwi fruit and pineapple; chop coarsely. Blend or process fruit and remaining ingredients, in batches, until smooth.

makes 1.25 litres (5 cups)

per cup 0.8g fat; 265kJ
tip You will need about 4 passionfruit for this recipe.

peach smoothie

PREPARATION TIME 10 MINUTES

- 825g can peaches in natural juice, drained
- ½ cup (125ml) yogurt
- 1 tablespoon honey
- 12 ice cubes
- 2 cups (500ml) milk

1 Blend or process ingredients until smooth.

makes 6 cups

per cup 3.9g fat; 657kJ

thailand

The flavours of Thai food vary from fragrantly aromatic to fiery hot.
Spicy red and green curry pastes, tangy fish sauce, and an
abundance of fresh coriander, lemon grass and basil are
teamed with seafood, chicken, meat, vegetables and noodles
in a fresh, light cuisine that's become a favourite around the world.

tom ka gai

PREPARATION TIME 20 MINUTES ■ COOKING TIME 30 MINUTES

2 teaspoons peanut oil

**1 tablespoon finely chopped fresh
lemon grass**

1 tablespoon grated fresh galangal

2 teaspoons grated fresh ginger

1 clove garlic, crushed

**3 fresh red thai chillies, seeded,
chopped finely**

4 kaffir lime leaves, sliced thinly

¼ teaspoon ground turmeric

2²/₃ cups (660ml) coconut milk

1 litre (4 cups) chicken stock

2 cups (500ml) water

1 tablespoon fish sauce

**500g chicken thigh fillets,
sliced thinly**

3 green onions, chopped finely

2 tablespoons lime juice

**1 tablespoon coarsely chopped
fresh coriander**

1 Heat oil in large saucepan; cook lemon grass, galangal, ginger, garlic, chilli, lime leaves and turmeric, stirring, about 2 minutes or until fragrant.

2 Stir in coconut milk, stock, the water and sauce; bring to a boil. Add chicken; reduce heat. Simmer, uncovered, about 20 minutes or until chicken is cooked through and soup liquid reduces slightly.

3 Just before serving, stir onion, juice and coriander into soup.

serves 6

per serving 30.8g fat; 1657kJ
tip Remove excess fat from chicken before cooking.

tom yum goong

PREPARATION TIME 20 MINUTES ■ COOKING TIME 2 HOURS

1kg fish bones

3 litres (12 cups) cold water

1 tablespoon peanut oil

**2 medium brown onions (300g),
chopped finely**

**2 trimmed sticks celery (150g),
chopped finely**

**2 sticks fresh lemon grass,
chopped finely**

**5 kaffir lime leaves,
chopped coarsely**

4 fresh red thai chillies, sliced thinly

2 tablespoons grated fresh ginger

**1 tablespoon finely grated
fresh galangal**

2 teaspoons fish sauce

24 large uncooked prawns (1kg)

80g bean sprouts, tips trimmed

2 green onions, sliced thinly

**½ cup loosely packed
fresh coriander**

**¼ cup loosely packed fresh
vietnamese mint**

1 Combine bones and the water in large saucepan; cover. Bring to a boil; reduce heat. Simmer, uncovered, 20 minutes. Strain fish stock over large bowl; discard bones. *[Can be made a day ahead to this stage and refrigerated, covered, or frozen for up to 3 months.]*

2 Heat oil in large saucepan; cook brown onion, stirring, until soft. Add celery, lemon grass, lime leaves, chilli, ginger, galangal and sauce; cook, stirring, about 5 minutes or until mixture is fragrant and celery is tender. Add reserved fish stock; bring to a boil. Reduce heat; simmer, covered, 1½ hours.

3 Strain stock mixture through muslin cloth over large bowl; discard solids.

4 Meanwhile, shell and devein prawns, leaving tails intact.

5 Return stock to cleaned large saucepan. Cover; bring to a boil. Reduce heat; simmer, uncovered, 20 minutes. Add prawns; cook, uncovered, about 5 minutes or until prawns just change colour.

6 Just before serving, stir in sprouts, green onion, coriander and mint.

serves 4

per serving 7g fat; 1018kJ

green
lamb curry

PREPARATION TIME 10 MINUTES ▪ COOKING TIME 1 HOUR 45 MINUTES

1 tablespoon vegetable oil
1kg diced lamb
1 large brown onion (200g), sliced thinly
1/3 cup (80g) green curry paste
3 cups (750ml) chicken stock
2 bay leaves
1$2/3$ cups (410ml) coconut cream
1 large green capsicum (350g), sliced thinly
100g snow peas, trimmed
425g can whole baby corn, drained
2 tablespoons finely chopped fresh coriander
1/2 cup (40g) bean sprouts

1 Heat oil in large saucepan. Cook lamb, in batches, until browned all over; remove from pan. Cook onion and paste in pan, stirring, until onion is soft. Return lamb to pan; add stock and bay leaves. Bring to a boil; reduce heat. Simmer, uncovered, 1$1/2$ hours or until lamb is tender. *[Can be made a day ahead to this stage and refrigerated, covered, or frozen for up to 3 months.]*

2 Add coconut cream, capsicum, snow peas, corn and coriander; stir until heated through. Serve topped with sprouts.

serves 4

per serving 50.6g fat; 3325kJ

chicken larb

PREPARATION TIME 20 MINUTES ■ COOKING TIME 15 MINUTES

2 tablespoons peanut oil

1 tablespoon finely chopped
   fresh lemon grass

2 fresh red thai chillies, seeded,
   chopped finely

1 clove garlic, crushed

1 tablespoon grated fresh ginger

750g minced chicken

4 kaffir lime leaves

1 tablespoon fish sauce

1/3 cup (80ml) lime juice

1 medium white onion (150g),
   sliced thinly

1 cup loosely packed fresh coriander

100g bean sprouts, tips trimmed

1/2 cup loosely packed fresh
   thai basil

1/2 cup loosely packed fresh
   vietnamese mint

100g watercress

1 lebanese cucumber (130g),
   sliced thinly

1 tablespoon finely chopped fresh
   vietnamese mint, extra

1 Heat half of the oil in large saucepan; cook lemon grass, chilli, garlic and ginger, stirring, until fragrant. Add chicken; cook, stirring, about 10 minutes or until cooked through.

2 Add torn lime leaves, half of the sauce and half of the juice; cook, stirring, 5 minutes.

3 Combine onion, coriander, sprouts, basil, mint, watercress and cucumber in large bowl. Drizzle with combined remaining oil, sauce and juice; toss salad mixture gently.

4 Place salad mixture on serving plate; top with chicken mixture. Sprinkle with extra mint.

serves 4

per serving 17.7g fat; 1446kJ

tip Add minced chicken to pan in batches, stirring between additions, so chicken doesn't clump. Minced beef or pork can be substituted for chicken, if preferred.

beef salad
with chilli dressing

PREPARATION TIME 20 MINUTES (plus standing time) ■ COOKING TIME 10 MINUTES

500g beef scotch fillet

2 medium tomatoes (380g), seeded, sliced thinly

2 lebanese cucumbers (260g), sliced thinly

4 golden shallots (50g), sliced thinly

¼ cup loosely packed fresh thai basil

¼ cup loosely packed fresh spearmint

¼ cup loosely packed fresh coriander

chilli dressing

1 fresh red thai chilli, sliced thinly

1 clove garlic, crushed

2 tablespoons palm sugar

1 tablespoon fish sauce

1 tablespoon soy sauce

¼ cup (60ml) lime juice

1 Sear beef on heated oiled grill plate (or grill or barbecue) over high heat until browned on both sides; beef should be rare. Stand beef, covered, 10 minutes; slice thinly.

2 Just before serving, place beef in large bowl with tomato, cucumber, shallot, basil, mint and coriander. Add chilli dressing; toss to combine.

chilli dressing Combine ingredients in small bowl. *[Can be made a day ahead and refrigerated, covered.]*

serves 4

per serving 7.7g fat; 1001kJ

tip Thai basil, also known as holy basil or krapow, is different from European basil. If you cannot find it, simply increase the quantities of mint and coriander to compensate.

mee krob

PREPARATION TIME 20 MINUTES ■ COOKING TIME 20 MINUTES

vegetable oil, for deep-frying
125g dried rice noodles
1½ tablespoons peanut oil
2 eggs, beaten lightly
1 tablespoon water
500g minced chicken
¼ cup (60ml) lemon juice
2 tablespoons fish sauce
2 tablespoons tomato sauce
1 teaspoon soy sauce
2 tablespoons brown sugar
2 teaspoons finely chopped fresh red thai chillies
1 tablespoon finely chopped fresh coriander
3 green onions, sliced thinly
300g firm tofu, chopped coarsely

1 Heat vegetable oil in large saucepan; deep-fry noodles, in batches, until puffed. Drain noodles on absorbent paper.

2 Heat 1 teaspoon of the peanut oil in large wok or frying pan; pour in half of the combined egg and water. Swirl pan to make a thin omelette; cook until just set. Transfer omelette to chopping board. Roll tightly; cut into thin strips. Repeat with 1 more teaspoon of vegetable oil and remaining egg mixture.

3 Heat remaining oil in wok; stir-fry chicken until browned and cooked. Add combined juice, sauces, sugar, chilli and coriander; stir-fry 1 minute. Add onion, tofu and omelette strips; stir-fry until heated through. Just before serving, gently toss noodles through chicken mixture.

serves 4

per serving 29.1g fat; 2294kJ

creamy chicken
and basil curry

PREPARATION TIME 15 MINUTES ■ COOKING TIME 40 MINUTES

750g chicken thigh fillets

2 tablespoons peanut oil

1 tablespoon grated fresh galangal

3¹/4 cups (810ml) coconut milk

1 tablespoon fish sauce

¹/4 cup fresh basil, torn

green curry paste

8 small fresh green thai chillies, chopped coarsely

3 cloves garlic, chopped coarsely

2 stalks fresh lemon grass, chopped coarsely

3 fresh coriander roots and stems, chopped coarsely

2 teaspoons grated lime rind

1 teaspoon caraway seeds

1 teaspoon ground turmeric

1 teaspoon shrimp paste

2 tablespoons water

1 Cut chicken into 1cm-thick strips.

2 Heat oil in large saucepan; cook 2 tablespoons of the green curry paste, stirring, over high heat 1 minute. Add chicken to pan; stir over medium heat about 3 minutes or until chicken is well coated in curry paste and browned lightly all over.

3 Add galangal. Stir in coconut milk; bring to a boil. Reduce heat; simmer, uncovered, about 45 minutes or until mixture is thick. Stir in sauce; sprinkle with basil.

green curry paste Blend or process ingredients until chopped finely.

serves 4

per serving 64.1g fat; 3195kJ

tip Curry paste will keep for 2 weeks in jar in refrigerator. Curry is best made close to serving time.

peanut lamb curry

PREPARATION TIME 35 MINUTES (plus standing time) ■ COOKING TIME 20 MINUTES

000g lamb fillets

1 tablespoon oil

3 fresh red thai chillies, chopped finely

1½ cups (375ml) coconut milk

2 tablespoons fish sauce

1 teaspoon palm sugar

2 tablespoons lime juice

½ cup (75g) unsalted roasted peanuts, chopped finely

2 tablespoons finely chopped fresh coriander

curry paste

2 fresh red thai chillies, chopped finely

1 dried kaffir lime leaf

½ teaspoon galangal powder

1 stem fresh lemon grass, chopped finely

1 teaspoon shrimp powder

⅓ cup (80ml) boiling water

4 green onions, chopped finely

2 cloves garlic, crushed

¼ teaspoon ground coriander

1 tablespoon fish sauce

2 tablespoons crunchy peanut butter

1 Cut each lamb fillet into three portions; using meat mallet, pound each piece until 5mm thick. Heat oil in large saucepan. Cook lamb until browned on both sides; remove from pan.

2 Combine 2 tablespoons of the curry paste with chilli in pan; stir over heat about 2 minutes or until fragrant.

3 Add coconut milk, sauce, sugar, juice and nuts; stir until boiling. Return lamb to pan; simmer, covered, about 5 minutes or until lamb is tender. Stir in coriander.

curry paste Combine chilli, lime leaf, galangal, lemon grass, shrimp powder and the water in medium heatproof bowl; stand 20 minutes. Drain chilli mixture; discard liquid. Blend or process chilli mixture with remaining ingredients until mixture forms a coarse paste.

serves 4

per serving 49g fat; 2865kJ

tip Recipe can be made 3 hours ahead and refrigerated, covered; paste can be made 2 weeks ahead and refrigerated, covered. Recipe can be frozen for up to a month.

phad thai

PREPARATION TIME 25 MINUTES ■ COOKING TIME 20 MINUTES

375g rice stick noodles
¼ cup (65g) palm sugar
2 teaspoons soy sauce
1 tablespoon tomato sauce
¼ cup (60ml) sweet chilli sauce
¼ cup (60ml) fish sauce
1 tablespoon peanut oil
200g minced pork
2 cloves garlic, crushed
1 tablespoon grated fresh ginger
3 eggs, beaten lightly
200g medium cooked prawns, shelled
2 teaspoons finely chopped fresh red thai chillies
2 green onions, sliced thinly
160g bean sprouts, tips trimmed
2 tablespoons finely chopped fresh coriander
½ cup (75g) unsalted roasted peanuts, chopped coarsely

1 Place noodles in large heatproof bowl; cover with boiling water. Stand until just tender; drain. Cover to keep warm.

2 Combine sugar and sauces in small saucepan; cook, stirring, until sugar dissolves.

3 Heat oil in heated large wok or frying pan; stir-fry pork, garlic and ginger until pork is browned and almost cooked. Add egg and prawns; stir-fry until egg sets.

4 Add noodles, sauce mixture and remaining ingredients; gently stir-fry until heated through.

serves 6

per serving 15.2g fat; 1870kJ

corn soup with
fish cakes

PREPARATION TIME 25 MINUTES (plus refrigeration time) ■ COOKING TIME 35 MINUTES

8 corn cobs (3.2kg)

1 tablespoon peanut oil

1 large brown onion (200g), chopped finely

2 cloves garlic, crushed

1 tablespoon grated fresh ginger

⅓ cup coarsely chopped fresh lemon grass

500g pumpkin, chopped coarsely

3 cups (750ml) vegetable stock

1.5 litres (6 cups) water

fish cakes

2 green onions, chopped coarsely

2 tablespoons coarsely chopped fresh coriander

400g boneless firm white fish fillets, chopped coarsely

2 tablespoons torn fresh vietnamese mint

1 fresh red thai chilli, quartered

1 egg

4 kaffir lime leaves, torn

1 tablespoon thinly sliced fresh ginger

2 cloves garlic, quartered

2 tablespoons peanut oil

1 Cut kernels from corn cobs; discard cobs.

2 Heat oil in large saucepan; cook onion, garlic, ginger and lemon grass, stirring, until onion softens. Add corn and pumpkin; cook, stirring, 5 minutes.

3 Add stock and the water; bring to a boil. Reduce heat; simmer, covered, about 20 minutes or until pumpkin is tender.

4 Blend or process soup mixture, in batches, until pureed. Push soup through food mill or large sieve into cleaned pan; stir over heat until hot. *[Can be made a day ahead and refrigerated, covered, or frozen for up to 3 months.]* Serve soup with fish cakes; sprinkle with extra chopped coriander, if desired.

fish cakes Process onion, coriander, fish, mint, chilli, egg, lime leaves, ginger and garlic until combined. Using hands, roll level tablespoons of fish mixture into balls; shape balls into patty-shaped cakes (you will have 18 fish cakes). Place fish cakes on tray. Cover; refrigerate 30 minutes. *[Can be made a day ahead to this stage or frozen for up to 3 months.]* Heat oil in large frying pan; cook fish cakes, in batches, until browned on both sides and cooked through. Drain on absorbent paper.

serves 6

per serving 15g fat; 1815kJ

tip Kumara can be substituted for pumpkin, if desired.

thai-crusted chicken
salad

PREPARATION TIME 15 MINUTES ■ COOKING TIME 20 MINUTES

**1 cup (150g) unsalted
roasted peanuts**

¼ cup (60g) red curry paste

1 cup loosely packed fresh coriander

⅓ cup (80ml) coconut milk

4 chicken breast fillets (700g)

1 large green cucumber (400g)

1 cup (80g) bean sprouts

⅓ cup loosely packed fresh mint

**1 medium red onion (170g),
sliced thinly**

1 Blend or process nuts, paste, half of the coriander and coconut milk until just combined and nuts are chopped coarsely.

2 Place chicken in oiled baking dish; spread a quarter of the paste mixture over top of each fillet. Bake, uncovered, in moderate oven about 20 minutes or until topping is browned and chicken cooked through. Stand chicken 5 minutes before cutting into thick slices.

3 Meanwhile, cut cucumber in half lengthways. Remove and discard seeds; slice thinly.

4 Combine chicken and cucumber with sprouts, mint, remaining coriander and onion in large bowl.

serves 4

per serving 31.9g fat; 2239kJ

musaman beef
curry

PREPARATION TIME 25 MINUTES (plus cooling time) ■ COOKING TIME 1 HOUR 10 MINUTES

1/4 cup (60ml) peanut oil

1kg beef topside steak, cut into
   3cm cubes

500g small potatoes, halved

250g small brown onions, halved

3¹/4 cups (810ml) coconut cream

1 teaspoon thick
   tamarind concentrate

2/3 cup (160ml) hot water

1/4 cup (50g) brown sugar

musaman curry paste

3 green onions, chopped coarsely

2 cloves garlic, crushed

2 tablespoons finely chopped
   fresh lemon grass

2 fresh red thai chillies,
   chopped finely

1 tablespoon coriander seeds

1 tablespoon cumin seeds

3 cardamom pods

1/2 teaspoon ground nutmeg

1/4 teaspoon ground cloves

1/4 teaspoon black peppercorns

2 teaspoons shrimp paste

1/4 cup (60ml) warm water

1 Heat oil in large saucepan; cook beef, stirring, over high heat until beef is browned all over. Remove beef from pan; drain on absorbent paper.

2 Cook potato and onion in pan; stir over high heat until browned lightly. Stir in musaman curry paste; stir over heat 1 minute.

3 Stir in coconut cream, then stir in beef and combined tamarind concentrate, water and sugar; bring to a boil. Reduce heat; simmer, uncovered, about 45 minutes or until beef is tender and mixture is thickened.

musaman curry paste Combine onion, garlic, lemon grass, chilli, seeds, cardamom, nutmeg, cloves and peppercorns in small bowl; sprinkle onto oven tray. Bake in moderate oven 10 minutes; cool. Blend or process shrimp paste and the water until combined. Gradually add spice mixture; blend or process until chopped finely. *[Can be made 2 weeks ahead and refrigerated, covered.]*

serves 6

per serving 42.6g fat; 2743kJ

tip Curry can be made 2 days ahead and refrigerated, covered, or frozen for up to 2 months.

green chicken curry

PREPARATION TIME 10 MINUTES ■ COOKING TIME 15 MINUTES

1 large white onion (200g), chopped finely

1 tablespoon grated fresh ginger

4 fresh kaffir lime leaves, shredded finely

10cm stem fresh lemon grass, bruised

2 tablespoons green curry paste

500g chicken thigh fillets, quartered

1 cup (250ml) chicken stock

1 cup (250ml) light coconut milk

1 small green capsicum (120g), sliced thinly

1 cup (140g) shelled peas

¼ cup (15g) firmly packed fresh purple basil, torn

¼ cup (15g) firmly packed fresh coriander, torn

1 Combine onion, ginger, lime leaves, lemon grass and paste in large saucepan; stir over high heat 2 minutes.

2 Add chicken, stock and coconut milk; bring slowly to a boil. Reduce heat; simmer, uncovered, 10 minutes. Add capsicum and peas, cook further 3 minutes or until chicken and vegetables are tender.

3 Discard lemon grass. Carefully stir in basil and coriander.

serves 4

per serving 12g fat; 1356kJ

fish with coriander chilli sauce

PREPARATION TIME 10 MINUTES ■ COOKING TIME 25 MINUTES

6 x 70g ocean perch fillets

1 small brown onion (80g), sliced thinly

½ cup (125ml) water

¼ cup (60ml) dry vermouth

2 tablespoons lime juice

1 fresh red thai chilli, chopped finely

2 tablespoons sugar

1 teaspoon cornflour

1 tablespoon finely chopped fresh coriander

½ medium red capsicum (100g), sliced thinly

2 green onions, cut into 5cm lengths

¼ cup firmly packed fresh coriander, extra

1 Place fish in shallow ovenproof dish; top with brown onion. Pour over combined water, vermouth and 1 tablespoon of the juice; cover. Bake in moderate oven about 15 minutes or until fish is tender.

2 Remove fish; keep warm. Strain and reserve liquid.

3 Place reserved liquid, chilli, sugar and combined cornflour and remaining juice in small saucepan.

4 Stir over heat until sugar dissolves. Bring to a boil; boil until mixture thickens. Stir in chopped coriander. Arrange fish, capsicum, green onion and extra coriander on serving plates; drizzle with sauce.

serves 2

per serving 4.8g fat; 1453kJ

pork curry with eggplant

PREPARATION TIME 30 MINUTES ■ COOKING TIME 20 MINUTES

750g pork fillets

1/4 cup (60ml) coconut cream

2 1/2 cups (625ml) coconut milk

**1 medium eggplant (300g),
    chopped coarsely**

1 tablespoon fish sauce

1 1/2 teaspoons grated fresh ginger

2 teaspoons palm sugar

**3 fresh green thai chillies,
    sliced thinly**

3 fresh red thai chillies, sliced thinly

1/4 cup fresh basil leaves, torn

curry paste

2 teaspoons dried chilli flakes

**1 medium red onion (170g),
    chopped finely**

3 cloves garlic, crushed

**2 tablespoons finely chopped fresh
    lemon grass**

1 teaspoon galangal powder

**2 teaspoons finely chopped fresh
    coriander root**

1 teaspoon grated lime rind

1/2 teaspoon shrimp paste

1 dried kaffir lime leaf

1 teaspoon paprika

1/2 teaspoon ground turmeric

1/2 teaspoon cumin seeds

2 teaspoons oil, approximately

1 Cut pork into 2cm slices; cut slices in half. Combine coconut cream and curry paste in large saucepan; cook about 1 minute or until fragrant. Add pork; cook 5 minutes.

2 Stir in coconut milk, eggplant, sauce, ginger, sugar and chillies; bring to a boil. Reduce heat; simmer, covered, until pork is tender. Stir in basil.

curry paste Blend or process ingredients with enough of the oil for mixture to form a paste.

serves 6

per serving 30.3g fat; 1790kJ

tip Recipe can be prepared a day ahead; paste can be made a week ahead and refrigerated, covered.

lime and tamarind **bream**

PREPARATION TIME 20 MINUTES ▧ COOKING TIME 30 MINUTES

2 tablespoons thick tamarind concentrate

1/3 cup (80ml) boiling water

2 cloves garlic, crushed

1 tablespoon grated fresh ginger

2 tablespoons lime juice

2 fresh red thai chillies, seeded, chopped finely

2 tablespoons finely chopped fresh lemon grass

16 kaffir lime leaves, torn

4 medium whole bream (1.8kg)

1/4 cup loosely packed fresh coriander

2 fresh red thai chillies, sliced thinly, extra

1 Combine tamarind concentrate and the water in medium heatproof bowl; stir in garlic, ginger, juice, chilli and lemon grass.

2 Divide lime leaves among fish cavities. Score fish on both sides; brush with a third of the tamarind mixture.

3 Wrap each fish in oiled foil; place on oven tray. Cook in moderately hot oven about 30 minutes or until fish is cooked through, brushing with more of the tamarind mixture during cooking. Serve fish topped with coriander and extra chilli; accompany with steamed rice, if desired.

serves 4

per serving 11.7g fat; 1207kJ

tips Use tamarind pulp if you cannot find the concentrate – soak 100g tamarind pulp in 1/2 cup (125ml) hot water 10 minutes. Squeeze pulp to release extra flavour; strain. Use liquid; discard pulp.

You can use any small, whole, white-fleshed fish for this recipe.

tofu and egg salad

PREPARATION TIME 25 MINUTES (plus cooling and standing time) ■ COOKING TIME 15 MINUTES

2 teaspoons coarsely chopped fresh coriander root

1 clove garlic, crushed

1 tablespoon grated fresh ginger

2 tablespoons brown sugar

2 tablespoons dark soy sauce

1 teaspoon five-spice powder

2 teaspoons oil

1/4 cup (60ml) water

6 radishes (200g)

375g firm tofu, drained, cubed

1 tablespoon finely chopped fresh coriander

1 fresh red thai chilli, chopped finely

1 hard-boiled egg, chopped coarsely

1 Blend coriander root, garlic, ginger, sugar, sauce and five-spice until well combined.

2 Heat oil in large wok or frying pan; cook ginger mixture, stirring, about 2 minutes or until fragrant. Stir in the water; cool to room temperature.

3 Cut radishes into thin strips. Combine tofu and radish in large bowl; pour over ginger mixture. Cover; stand 2 hours, stirring occasionally.

4 Drain tofu mixture; combine with coriander, chilli and egg.

serves 4

per serving 9.6g fat; 835kJ

tip Recipe can be prepared 6 hours ahead and refrigerated, covered.

stir-fried seafood
with basil

PREPARATION TIME 30 MINUTES ■ COOKING TIME 10 MINUTES

200g white fish fillets
8 mussels
250g uncooked king prawns
100g squid hoods
2 cloves garlic, crushed
1 fresh red dutch chilli, chopped finely
1 tablespoon finely chopped fresh coriander root
¼ cup (60ml) peanut oil
100g scallops
2 tablespoons oyster sauce
2 tablespoons fish sauce
1 medium red capsicum (200g), sliced thinly
8 green onions, chopped finely
⅓ cup shredded fresh basil

1 Cut fish into bite-sized pieces. Scrub mussels; remove beards. Shell prawns, leaving tails intact. Cut squid into 6cm squares; score inside surface of squid using sharp knife. *[Can be made a day ahead to this stage and refrigerated, covered.]*

2 Using mortar and pestle, grind garlic, chilli and coriander until mixture forms a paste. Heat oil in large wok or frying pan; cook paste stirring, about 1 minute or until fragrant.

3 Add all seafood to wok; stir-fry until tender.

4 Stir in sauces, capsicum, onion and basil; stir-fry 2 minutes. Serve with extra fresh basil and green onion curls, if desired.

serves 4

per serving 18g fat; 1406kJ

thai
red curry vegetables

PREPARATION TIME 20 MINUTES ■ COOKING TIME 20 MINUTES

1 tablespoon peanut oil

1 large leek (500g), sliced thinly

2 cloves garlic, crushed

1 large red thai chilli, seeded, chopped finely

1/3 cup (90g) thai red curry paste

2 medium carrots (240g), chopped coarsely

3 trimmed sticks celery (225g), sliced thinly

400g canned tomatoes

1²/3 cups (410ml) coconut cream

1 cup (250ml) vegetable stock

300g cauliflower, cut into florets

1 medium kumara (400g), cut into 3cm pieces

175g snake beans, chopped into 4cm lengths

4 kaffir lime leaves

1/4 cup coarsely chopped fresh coriander

1 Heat oil in large saucepan; cook leek, garlic and chilli, stirring, until leek is just soft.

2 Add paste to pan; cook, stirring, until mixture is fragrant. Add carrot and celery; cook, stirring, 5 minutes. Add undrained crushed tomatoes, coconut cream and stock; bring to a boil. Reduce heat; simmer, uncovered, 10 minutes.

3 Add cauliflower, kumara, beans and lime leaves; simmer, uncovered, further 15 minutes or until kumara is just tender. Stir through coriander; simmer, uncovered, about 5 minutes or until curry sauce thickens. Serve with steamed rice, if desired.

serves 4

per serving 30.6g fat; 1863kJ

tips Bean sprouts, bamboo shoots, tiny thai eggplant and peas can be used instead of (or with) the vegetables used here.

Kaffir lime leaves can be frozen in an airtight plastic bag.

sweet
puffed noodles

PREPARATION TIME 15 MINUTES ■ COOKING TIME 10 MINUTES

vegetable oil, for deep-frying
100g thin rice stick noodles
3 teaspoons peanut oil
2 cloves garlic, crushed
100g minced chicken
1 egg, beaten lightly
¼ cup (55g) sugar
2 tablespoons water
1 tablespoon white vinegar
300g small cooked prawns, shelled
2 green onions, sliced thinly

1 Heat oil in large wok or frying pan; deep-fry vermicelli in hot oil, in batches, until puffed. Drain on absorbent paper.

2 Heat 2 teaspoons of the peanut oil in small saucepan; cook garlic, stirring, 1 minute. Add chicken; cook, stirring, a further minute or until cooked. Remove from pan.

3 Heat remaining peanut oil in wok. Cook egg, swirling to coat base of pan, 1 minute on both sides; remove. Roll firmly; cut into 5mm-thick slices.

4 Combine sugar, the water and vinegar in small saucepan; stir over heat until sugar dissolves. Combine vermicelli, chicken mixture, prawns, onion, omelette strips and sugar syrup in large bowl; toss lightly.

serves 6

per serving 9g fat; 831.6kJ

octopus with lime and chilli

PREPARATION TIME 20 MINUTES (plus marinating time) ■ COOKING TIME 30 MINUTES

2kg cleaned baby octopus, halved

1/2 cup (125ml) olive oil

1/4 cup (60ml) dry red wine

1/4 cup finely chopped fresh lemon grass

2 tablespoons finely grated lime rind

1 tablespoon finely grated lemon rind

3 cloves garlic, crushed

4 fresh red thai chillies, seeded, chopped finely

2 teaspoons grated fresh ginger

1 cup (250ml) peanut oil

16 wonton wrappers

1 tablespoon sea salt

2 teaspoons chilli powder

1 medium leek (350g)

1 tablespoon sweet chilli sauce

1 Combine octopus, olive oil, wine, lemon grass, rinds, garlic, fresh chilli and ginger in large bowl. Cover; refrigerate 3 hours or until required. *[Can be made a day ahead to this stage.]*

2 Drain octopus over medium bowl; reserve 1/2 cup (125ml) of the marinade.

3 Heat peanut oil in large wok or frying pan. Shallow-fry wonton wrappers, in batches, until browned lightly; drain on absorbent paper. While still warm, sprinkle wrappers with combined salt and chilli powder.

4 Halve leek lengthways; cut halves into long thin strips.

5 Reheat peanut oil in wok. Deep-fry leek, in batches, until browned lightly; drain on absorbent paper.

6 Drain peanut oil from wok. Stir-fry octopus in wok, in batches, until tender.

7 Return octopus to wok with reserved marinade and chilli sauce; stir over high heat, tossing until sauce boils and thickens slightly.

8 Serve octopus, topped with leek, with chilli wrappers.

serves 6

per serving 27.3g fat; 2047kJ

lemon grass mussels

PREPARATION TIME 10 MINUTES ■ COOKING TIME 10 MINUTES

28 mussels (approximately 850g)

2 stalks fresh lemon grass

2 cloves garlic, crushed

2 fresh red thai chillies, seeded, chopped finely

¼ cup (60ml) lime juice

2 teaspoons fish sauce

¼ cup (60ml) water

2 teaspoons sugar

¼ cup loosely packed, coarsely chopped fresh coriander

1 Scrub mussels under cold running water; remove beards.

2 Cut lemon grass into 5cm-long thin strips. Combine lemon grass, garlic, chilli, juice, sauce, the water and sugar in large saucepan; stir over heat, without boiling, until sugar dissolves. Bring to a boil; add mussels. Reduce heat; simmer, covered, about 5 minutes or until mussels open (discard any mussels that do not open). Serve sprinkled with coriander.

serves 4

per serving 1.1g fat; 235kJ

red chicken curry

PREPARATION TIME 15 MINUTES ■ COOKING TIME 40 MINUTES

750g chicken thigh fillets

1²/₃ cups (410ml) coconut milk

200g thai eggplants, halved

4 kaffir lime leaves, torn

1 medium red capsicum (200g), chopped coarsely

curry paste

3 cloves garlic, chopped coarsely

2 tablespoons coarsely chopped fresh lemon grass

1 tablespoon grated fresh galangal

4 green onions, chopped coarsely

1 teaspoon shrimp paste

5 fresh red thai chillies, seeded, chopped coarsely

1 teaspoon hot paprika

¼ cup (60ml) peanut oil

1 Cut chicken into 3cm-thick slices. Cook curry paste in heated large frying pan about 3 minutes or until fragrant. Add chicken; cook, stirring, until browned. Stir in coconut milk, eggplant and lime leaves; bring to a boil. Reduce heat; simmer, uncovered, 20 minutes. *[Can be made 3 days ahead to this stage and refrigerated, covered.]*

2 Add capsicum; simmer, uncovered, about 10 minutes or until capsicum is just tender. Discard lime leaves before serving. Serve with steamed rice, if desired.

curry paste Blend or process ingredients until smooth.

serves 4

per serving 45.8g fat; 2510kJ

tip Green beans can be substituted for thai eggplants, if unavailable.

mermaid's tresses

PREPARATION TIME 30 MINUTES
COOKING TIME 10 MINUTES

1kg chinese broccoli
2 teaspoons brown sugar
2 teaspoons water
½ cup (75g) roasted unsalted cashews
2 teaspoons white sesame seeds
vegetable oil, for deep-frying
2 tablespoons small dried shrimp
1 teaspoon sugar
½ teaspoon salt

1 Trim stems and hard veins from broccoli; shred broccoli leaves finely.

2 Combine brown sugar and the water in medium saucepan; cook, stirring, until sugar dissolves. Add nuts and seeds; cook, stirring, until coated in sugar mixture. Place on oiled oven tray; cool.

3 Heat oil in large wok or frying pan. Deep-fry shrimp until crisp; drain on absorbent paper. Deep-fry broccoli, in batches, until crisp. Drain on absorbent paper; sprinkle with combined sugar and salt. Place mermaid's tresses in serving bowl; sprinkle with nut mixture and shrimp.

serves 6

per serving 15.6g fat; 750kJ
tip Ensure broccoli is completely dry before deep-frying or it will make the oil splatter.

japanese cucumber salad

PREPARATION TIME 25 MINUTES (plus standing time)
COOKING TIME 10 MINUTES

2 large green cucumbers (800g)
1 tablespoon coarse cooking salt
⅓ cup (80ml) mirin
¼ cup (60ml) rice vinegar
1 tablespoon soy sauce
1 tablespoon dashi
2 teaspoons sugar
vegetable oil, for deep-frying
300g firm tofu, cut into 3cm cubes
2 teaspoons shredded wakame

1 Cut cucumbers in half lengthways. Remove seeds, cut into thin slices. Combine cucumber and salt in large bowl. Cover; refrigerate 30 minutes. [Can be made 3 hours ahead to this stage.]

2 Meanwhile, combine mirin, vinegar, sauce, dashi and sugar in small saucepan. Stir over heat, without boiling, about 5 minutes or until sugar dissolves; cool.

3 Heat oil in medium saucepan; deep-fry tofu, in batches, until browned. Drain on absorbent paper.

4 Rinse cucumber under cold running water; drain.

5 Just before serving, combine cucumber, wakame and mirin mixture in medium bowl; toss gently to combine. Divide tofu among serving plates; top with cucumber salad.

serves 4

per serving 7.1g fat; 599kJ

cucumber and pineapple sambal

PREPARATION TIME 15 MINUTES
COOKING TIME 2 MINUTES

- **3 teaspoons shrimp paste**
- **2 fresh red thai chillies, seeded, chopped finely**
- **1 tablespoon lime juice**
- **1 tablespoon soy sauce**
- **1 teaspoon sugar**
- **1 small green cucumber (130g), peeled, seeded, chopped coarsely**
- **1 small pineapple (800g), chopped coarsely**
- **6 green onions, sliced thinly**

1 Cook paste in dry large saucepan until dry and crumbly. Combine paste and chilli in small bowl; grind with mortar and pestle. Stir in juice, sauce and sugar; mix well.

2 Combine cucumber, pineapple and onion in large bowl; stir in chilli mixture.

serves 6

per serving 0.3g fat; 230kJ
tip Recipe can be made a day ahead and refrigerated, covered.

carrot and mustard seed salad

PREPARATION TIME 10 MINUTES
COOKING TIME 10 MINUTES

- **1 tablespoon black mustard seeds**
- **4 medium carrots (480g)**
- **1 tablespoon peanut oil**
- **1/4 cup (60ml) lemon juice**
- **1 large red onion (300g), chopped finely**
- **1/4 cup fresh coriander**

1 Cook mustard seeds in heated dry large frying pan, stirring, until fragrant. Halve carrots lengthways; cut each half diagonally into 2cm slices. Boil, steam or microwave carrot until tender. Drain; cool.

2 Just before serving, combine carrot with seeds and remaining ingredients; toss to combine.

serves 4

per serving 5.3g fat; 422kJ

salads

malaysia and singapore

The geographical proximity of these two countries and a shared heritage that includes Indian, Muslim and Chinese influences, means that they also share many dishes – laksa is perhaps the most famous. But each has its own regional specialties too – Singapore's famous chilli crab, for example, or richly spicy rendang curry from Malaysia.

shellfish laksa

PREPARATION TIME 45 MINUTES ■ COOKING TIME 30 MINUTES

8 medium cooked balmain bugs (1kg)

1 small leek (200g)

vegetable oil, for shallow-frying

16 large uncooked prawns (630g)

3 cups (750ml) water

1 tablespoon peanut oil

¾ cup (210g) laksa paste

3 cups (750ml) coconut milk

8 kaffir lime leaves, torn

2 teaspoons fish sauce

200g thin fresh egg noodles

1 small red capsicum (150g), sliced thinly

100g bean sprouts, tips trimmed

50g snow peas, sliced thinly

4 green onions, chopped finely

⅓ cup loosely packed fresh coriander

¼ cup (35g) coarsely chopped roasted cashews

1 Place balmain bugs, upside down, on chopping board. Cut tail from body; cut through tail lengthways. Remove back vein from tail; remove meat from tail halves.

2 Halve leek lengthways. Discard roots and green stem; cut white section into thin strips. Shallow-fry leek in vegetable oil, in batches, until browned lightly; drain on absorbent paper.

3 Shell and devein prawns, leaving tails intact.

4 Place the water in large saucepan; cover. Bring to a boil; add seafood. Reduce heat; simmer, uncovered, about 2 minutes or until just cooked. Drain seafood over large bowl; reserve stock.

5 Heat peanut oil in large saucepan; cook paste, stirring, 2 minutes. Add coconut milk, lime leaves and reserved stock; simmer, uncovered, 15 minutes. Stir in sauce and seafood; simmer about 2 minutes or until heated through.

6 Meanwhile, place noodles in large heatproof bowl; cover with boiling water. Stand until just tender; drain. Divide noodles among serving bowls; add capsicum, sprouts, snow peas and seafood mixture. Top with leek, onion, coriander and nuts.

serves 4

per serving 69.8g fat; 4236kJ

singapore noodles

PREPARATION TIME 30 MINUTES ■ COOKING TIME 15 MINUTES

250g dried thin egg noodles

2 tablespoons peanut oil

4 eggs, beaten lightly

3 cloves garlic, crushed

1 tablespoon grated fresh ginger

1 medium white onion (150g), sliced thinly

2 tablespoons mild curry paste

230g canned water chestnuts, drained, chopped coarsely

3 green onions, sliced thinly on the diagonal

200g chinese barbecued pork, sliced thinly

500g medium uncooked prawns, shelled, deveined

2 tablespoons light soy sauce

2 tablespoons oyster sauce

1 Cook noodles in large saucepan of boiling water, uncovered, until just tender; drain.

2 Meanwhile, heat half of the oil in heated large wok or heavy-based frying pan. Cook half of the egg; swirl wok to make a thin omelette. Remove omelette from wok; roll omelette. Cut into thin strips; repeat with remaining egg.

3 Heat remaining oil in wok; stir-fry garlic and ginger 1 minute. Add white onion and paste; stir-fry 2 minutes or until fragrant.

4 Add water chestnuts, green onion and pork; stir-fry about 2 minutes or until water chestnuts are browned lightly.

5 Add prawns; stir-fry until prawns just change colour. Add noodles, combined sauces and omelette; stir-fry, tossing, until sauce thickens and noodles are heated through.

serves 4

per serving 27.2g fat; 2658kJ

tofu and bok choy
laksa

PREPARATION TIME 25 MINUTES ■ COOKING TIME 50 MINUTES

450g hokkien noodles

300g firm tofu

1/4 cup (60ml) peanut oil

2 stalks fresh lemon grass, chopped finely

2 cups (500ml) vegetable stock

2 cups (500ml) water

3 3/4 cups (940ml) light coconut milk

8 fresh kaffir lime leaves, torn

2 tablespoons brown sugar

2 tablespoons soy sauce

3 fresh coriander roots

1kg baby bok choy, trimmed

350g snake beans, trimmed, cut into 5cm lengths

1/4 cup fresh coriander

120g bean sprouts, tips trimmed

4 green onions, sliced thinly

yellow curry paste

1 medium brown onion (150g), chopped coarsely

1 tablespoon finely chopped fresh ginger

4 cloves garlic, chopped finely

1 tablespoon yellow curry paste

1/4 cup (60ml) light coconut milk

1 Place noodles in large heatproof bowl; cover with boiling water. Stand until just tender; drain.

2 Cut tofu into bite-sized pieces. Heat 2 tablespoons of the oil in large saucepan; cook tofu until browned lightly on each side. Drain on absorbent paper; keep warm.

3 Heat remaining oil in pan; cook lemon grass and yellow curry paste, stirring, over low heat until fragrant.

4 Add stock, the water, coconut milk, lime leaves, sugar, sauce and coriander roots; bring to a boil. Reduce heat; simmer, covered, 30 minutes.

5 Strain soup into large heatproof bowl; reserve lime leaves. Remove leaves from bok choy; slice stalks thinly. Combine reserved lime leaves, bok choy stalks and leaves, and snake beans with soup in bowl.

6 Just before serving, return soup mixture to pan; stir over heat until vegetables are tender. Stir in noodles, tofu and coriander. Ladle laksa into serving bowls; top with sprouts and onion.

yellow curry paste Blend or process ingredients until smooth. *[Can be made 3 days ahead and refrigerated, covered, or frozen for up to a month.]*

serves 4

per serving 42.6g fat; 3323kJ

prawn laksa

PREPARATION TIME 30 MINUTES ■ COOKING TIME 10 MINUTES

1kg uncooked king prawns

160g bean thread noodles

1 lebanese cucumber (130g)

¼ cup (70g) laksa paste

1.25 litres (5 cups) chicken stock

1 cup (250ml) light coconut milk

150g snow peas, sliced thinly on the diagonal

2 tablespoons lime juice

100g bean sprouts, tips trimmed

⅓ cup coarsely chopped fresh mint

⅓ cup coarsely chopped fresh coriander

1 Peel and devein prawns, leaving tails intact.

2 Place noodles in small heatproof bowl; cover with boiling water. Stand until just tender; drain. Using vegetable peeler, shave long thin slices from cucumber.

3 Combine paste, stock and coconut milk in large saucepan. Bring to a boil; cook 1 minute. Add prawns and snow peas; cook 2 minutes or until prawns change colour. Stir in juice and sprouts.

4 Place noodles in serving bowls; spoon over prawns and stock mixture. Top with cucumber; sprinkle with mint and coriander.

serves 4

per serving 10g fat; 2400kJ

stir-fried
silverbeet and almonds

PREPARATION TIME 10 MINUTES ■ COOKING TIME 10 MINUTES

2 teaspoons peanut oil
1/3 cup (25g) flaked almonds
2 tablespoons sweet sherry
2 tablespoons soy sauce
2 tablespoons honey
1 clove garlic, crushed
1/2 teaspoon sesame oil
1kg silverbeet, trimmed
6 green onions, chopped coarsely

1 Heat peanut oil in heated large wok or frying pan. Stir-fry nuts until just browned; remove from wok. Cook sherry, sauce, honey, garlic and oil in wok until sauce boils.

2 Add silverbeet and onion; stir-fry, tossing until silverbeet just wilts. Serve silverbeet mixture with nuts sprinkled over the top.

serves 4

per serving 5.3g fat; 626kJ

hainan chicken rice

PREPARATION TIME 25 MINUTES ■ COOKING TIME 1 HOUR 20 MINUTES

4 single chicken breasts on bone (1kg)

1 teaspoon chinese rice wine

2 teaspoons soy sauce

2cm-piece fresh ginger, sliced thinly

1 clove garlic, sliced thinly

2 green onions, chopped finely

2 litres (8 cups) water

1 teaspoon sesame oil

¼ teaspoon salt

1 cup (200g) jasmine rice

1 lebanese cucumber (130g), sliced thinly

1 green onion, sliced thinly

chilli ginger sambal

4 fresh red thai chillies, chopped coarsely

1 clove garlic, chopped coarsely

2cm-piece fresh ginger, chopped coarsely

1 teaspoon sesame oil

1 teaspoon water

2 teaspoons lime juice

1 Rub chicken all over with combined rice wine and sauce. Gently slide ginger, garlic and onion under chicken skin.

2 Bring the water to a boil in large saucepan. Place chicken in the water. Turn off heat; turn chicken pieces. Stand chicken in the water 20 minutes. Remove chicken from pan; return liquid to a boil. Return chicken to pan; stand 20 minutes. Repeat the boiling, turning and standing 4 times.

3 Remove chicken from pan; remove and discard skin. Brush chicken all over with remaining sauce, oil and salt.

4 Return cooking liquid to a boil; boil, uncovered, until reduced by a half.

5 Meanwhile, rinse rice thoroughly under cold running water. Place rice in large saucepan; add enough water to cover rice by 2cm. Cover pan; bring to a boil. Stir several times to prevent rice sticking. When boiling, remove lid and continue to boil until tunnels appear in rice and all the water has evaporated or been absorbed; do not stir. Cover; stand rice 20 minutes. Stir with fork; stand, covered, further 10 minutes.

6 Cut chicken into pieces; serve with rice, cucumber and chilli ginger sambal. Accompany with a bowl of cooking liquid sprinkled with extra onion.

chilli ginger sambal Blend ingredients (or grind in a mortar and pestle) until combined. *[Can be made a day ahead and refrigerated, covered.]*

serves 4

per serving 20.6g fat; 2158kJ

lion heads

PREPARATION TIME 15 MINUTES (plus marinating time) ■ COOKING TIME 10 MINUTES

500g chicken mince

2 tablespoons black bean sauce

2 tablespoons plum sauce

2 green onions, chopped finely

1 cup (70g) stale breadcrumbs

1 clove garlic, crushed

¼ teaspoon five-spice powder

¼ cup (70g) canned creamed corn

150g rice vermicelli

vegetable oil, for deep-frying

sweet chilli dipping sauce

2 tablespoons sweet chilli sauce

1 tablespoon soy sauce

2 tablespoons water

1 Combine chicken, sauces, onion, breadcrumbs, garlic, five-spice and corn in large bowl. Roll level tablespoons of mixture into balls; place on tray. Cover; refrigerate 1 hour or overnight. *[Can be made a day ahead to this stage and refrigerated, covered, or frozen for up to a month.]*

2 Break vermicelli into short pieces in medium bowl; coat balls with vermicelli.

3 Heat oil in large saucepan. Deep-fry balls, in batches, until browned and cooked through; drain on absorbent paper. Serve lion heads with sweet chilli dipping sauce.

sweet chilli dipping sauce Combine ingredients in small bowl.

makes 40

per ball 2g fat; 219kJ

tip Cooked rice can be substituted for noodles, if preferred.

fish cutlets with coconut

PREPARATION TIME 10 MINUTES (plus cooling time) ■ COOKING TIME 25 MINUTES

2 tablespoons desiccated coconut

1 tablespoon coriander seeds

2 teaspoons cumin seeds

1 fresh red thai chilli, seeded, chopped finely

2 cloves garlic, crushed

1 teaspoon grated fresh ginger

2 tablespoons tamarind sauce

15g ghee

1 medium brown onion (150g), chopped finely

1½ cups (375ml) coconut cream

4 white fish cutlets (1kg)

1 Stir coconut in small frying pan over medium heat until browned lightly; remove from pan. Add seeds to pan; stir over medium heat about 2 minutes or until browned lightly. Remove from pan; cool.

2 Blend or process coconut, seeds, chilli, garlic, ginger and sauce until smooth and paste-like. *[Can be made a day ahead to this stage and refrigerated, covered.]*

3 Heat ghee in medium frying pan; cook onion, stirring over medium heat about 2 minutes or until onion is soft. Stir in coconut mixture; stir over medium heat 1 minute.

4 Stir in coconut cream; bring to a boil. Reduce heat; add fish. Simmer, uncovered, about 8 minutes or until fish is tender. Turn fish halfway through cooking time. Serve with steamed jasmine rice and sliced fresh chilli, if desired.

serves 4

per serving 31g fat; 2010kJ

curry kapitan
with roti jala

PREPARATION TIME 30 MINUTES ■ COOKING TIME 45 MINUTES

2 tablespoons vegetable oil

2 medium brown onions (300g),
    sliced thinly

1/4 cup (60ml) water

1.5kg chicken pieces

2 1/4 cups (560ml) coconut milk

1 cup (250ml) coconut cream

spice paste

10 fresh red thai chillies

4 cloves garlic

3 teaspoons grated fresh turmeric

2 teaspoons grated fresh galangal

2 teaspoons finely chopped fresh
    lemon grass

10 candlenuts

1 tablespoon ground cumin

roti jala

1 cup (150g) plain flour

1 1/2 cups (375ml) milk

1 egg

1   Heat oil in heated large wok or saucepan; cook onion, stirring, until soft. Stir in spice paste and the water; cook, stirring, until fragrant.

2   Add chicken and coconut milk; simmer, covered, 20 minutes. Remove lid; simmer, uncovered, further 30 minutes, stirring occasionally, or until chicken is tender. Stir in coconut cream; serve with roti jala.

spice paste   Blend or process ingredients until smooth. *[Can be made a week ahead and refrigerated, covered.]*

roti jala   Place flour in large bowl. Gradually stir in combined milk and egg; beat until smooth. Strain batter into jug to remove lumps and make pouring easier. Heat greased 24cm frying pan over medium heat. Pour about 1/4 cup (60ml) of the batter from jug into pan, moving jug back and forth so that pancake will have a lacy appearance. Cook until browned lightly underneath and cooked on top; transfer to greaseproof paper. Stand 1 minute; fold in half. Fold in half again to form a triangle. Repeat with remaining batter.

serves 6

per serving   64.7g fat; 3598kJ

tip   Chicken curry and roti jala can be made a day ahead and refrigerated, covered, separately.

snapper
in banana leaves

PREPARATION TIME 30 MINUTES ■ COOKING TIME 30 MINUTES

4 large banana leaves

4 whole small snapper (1.5kg)

2 tablespoons grated fresh ginger

**1/3 cup thinly sliced fresh
   lemon grass**

2 cloves garlic, crushed

1 tablespoon lime juice

2 tablespoons soy sauce

1/4 cup (60ml) sweet chilli sauce

1 teaspoon sesame oil

80g bean sprouts, tips trimmed

225g baby bok choy, chopped finely

**2 trimmed sticks celery (150g),
   sliced thinly**

4 green onions, chopped finely

1 Cut each banana leaf into a 35cm square. Using tongs, dip one leaf at a time into large saucepan of boiling water; remove immediately. Rinse under cold running water; dry thoroughly. Leaves should be soft and pliable.

2 Cut three slashes into each side of fish. Place each fish on a square of leaf; top with ginger and lemon grass. Combine garlic, juice, sauces and oil in small bowl; drizzle a little of the mixture over each fish. Fold leaves over fish; secure parcels with kitchen string.

3 Place parcels on barbecue, seam-side down. Cook in covered barbecue, using indirect heat, following manufacturer's instructions, about 25 minutes or until just cooked through (or bake in very hot oven about 30 minutes or until cooked through).

4 Combine sprouts, bok choy, celery and onion with remaining sauce mixture. Cook on heated oiled grill plate (or grill or barbecue), until just cooked and tender. Serve vegetable mixture with fish.

serves 4

per serving 7.6g fat; 925kJ

marinated
grilled prawns

PREPARATION TIME 20 MINUTES (plus marinating time) ■ COOKING TIME 10 MINUTES

20 large uncooked prawns (1kg)

1 medium brown onion (150g), chopped finely

½ cup (140g) plain yogurt

½ teaspoon ground turmeric

½ teaspoon chilli powder

1 tablespoon sweet paprika

1 teaspoon grated fresh ginger

2 cloves garlic, crushed

1 tablespoon lemon juice

1 Wash prawns; pat dry with absorbent paper. Remove heads and legs, leaving tails and body shells intact.

2 Blend or process onion, yogurt, turmeric, chilli, paprika, ginger, garlic and juice until smooth. Combine yogurt mixture and prawns in large bowl; mix well. Cover; refrigerate overnight.

3 Grill or barbecue prawns until tender, brushing occasionally with marinade during cooking.

serves 4

per serving 2.3g fat; 640kJ

tip Prawn shells are usually eaten in this recipe but shells can be removed before adding prawns to marinade, if preferred.

stir-fried
vegetables

PREPARATION TIME 15 MINUTES (plus standing time) ■ COOKING TIME 10 MINUTES

30g dried shiitake mushrooms
1 medium carrot (120g)
2 teaspoons vegetable oil
2 teaspoons sesame oil
1 medium brown onion (150g), sliced thinly
2 cloves garlic, crushed
1 teaspoon grated fresh ginger
1 cup (125g) frozen peas, thawed
150g snow peas, sliced thickly
1 medium red capsicum (200g), sliced thinly
1 medium yellow capsicum (200g), chopped coarsely
4 green onions, chopped coarsely
227g can bamboo shoots, drained
1½ tablespoons soy sauce
3 teaspoons oyster sauce
1½ tablespoons hoisin sauce
3 teaspoons sweet chilli sauce

1 Place mushrooms in medium heatproof bowl; cover with boiling water. Stand 20 minutes; drain mushrooms. Discard stems; slice caps. Halve carrot; cut into thick sticks. Boil, steam or microwave carrot until just tender.

2 Heat oils in heated large wok or frying pan; cook brown onion, garlic and ginger, stirring, until onion is soft. Add mushrooms, carrot, peas, snow peas, capsicums, green onion and bamboo shoots; cook, stirring, until vegetables are just tender. Add combined sauces; cook, stirring, until heated through.

serves 4

per serving 5.7g fat; 629kJ

caramelised chicken
and noodles

PREPARATION TIME 15 MINUTES ■ COOKING TIME 15 MINUTES

400g thin dried wheat noodles

2 tablespoons vegetable oil

4 chicken breast fillets (680g), sliced thinly

5 cloves garlic, crushed

1 tablespoon finely chopped fresh ginger

2 tablespoons finely chopped fresh lemon grass

4 fresh red thai chillies, seeded, chopped finely

1/3 cup (60g) palm sugar

2 tablespoons water

1/4 cup (60ml) oyster sauce

2 tablespoons fish sauce

2 teaspoons thick tamarind concentrate

1/4 cup (60ml) lime juice

1/4 cup coarsely chopped fresh coriander

1 Cook noodles in large saucepan of boiling water, uncovered, until just tender; drain. Heat half of the oil in heated large wok or frying pan; stir-fry chicken, in batches, until browned and tender. Cover to keep warm.

2 Add remaining oil to wok; stir-fry garlic, ginger, lemon grass and chilli until fragrant. Stir in sugar and the water; cook, stirring, until sugar caramelises.

3 Return chicken to wok; stir-fry until coated in caramelised sugar mixture. Stir in noodles with combined sauces, tamarind and juice. Simmer until sauce thickens slightly.

4 Just before serving, sprinkle with coriander.

serves 4

per serving 20g fat; 3072kJ

dry squid curry

PREPARATION TIME 15 MINUTES ■ COOKING TIME 10 MINUTES

500g squid hoods

2 tablespoons mild chilli powder

1 teaspoon ground turmeric

1 tablespoon thick tamarind concentrate

2 tablespoons hot water

2 tablespoons vegetable oil

2 medium white onions (300g), chopped finely

4 cloves garlic, crushed

2 tablespoons tomato sauce

1 teaspoon soy sauce

1 tablespoon fish sauce

½ teaspoon sugar

⅓ cup (80ml) lemon juice

2 tablespoons packaged fried onions

1 Cut squid into rings. Combine squid, chilli powder and turmeric in large bowl; mix well. Place tamarind concentrate and the water in small bowl.

2 Heat oil in large frying pan. Cook squid mixture, stirring, until squid changes colour; remove from pan.

3 Cook onion and garlic in pan, stirring, until onion is soft. Add tamarind mixture, sauces and sugar; cook, stirring occasionally, 4 minutes.

4 Return squid to pan. Add juice; stir over heat until squid is tender. Serve sprinkled with fried onions.

serves 4

per serving 11.7g fat; 1030kJ

tip Recipe can be made a day ahead and refrigerated, covered.

chilli crab

PREPARATION TIME 20 MINUTES ■ COOKING TIME 20 MINUTES

4 medium uncooked blue swimmer crabs (3kg)
1 tablespoon peanut oil
2 fresh red thai chillies, seeded, chopped finely
1 tablespoon grated fresh ginger
2 cloves garlic, crushed
2 teaspoons fish sauce
25g palm sugar, chopped finely
¼ cup (60ml) lime juice
¼ cup (60ml) rice vinegar
¼ cup (60ml) fish stock
3 green onions, sliced thickly
¼ cup tightly packed fresh coriander

1 Prepare crab, leaving flesh in claws and legs. Chop each crab body into quarters with cleaver or strong sharp knife.

2 Heat oil in heated large wok or frying pan; cook chilli, ginger, garlic, sauce, sugar, juice, vinegar and stock, stirring, until sugar dissolves.

3 Add crab; cook, covered, about 15 minutes or until crab changes colour. Stir in onion and coriander.

serves 4

per serving 6.1g fat; 806kJ
tip Prawns can be substituted for crab in this recipe, if preferred.

char kway teow

PREPARATION TIME 15 MINUTES ■ COOKING TIME 10 MINUTES

1kg fresh rice noodle sheets

500g small uncooked prawns

¼ cup (60ml) peanut oil

2 chicken breast fillets (340g), chopped coarsely

4 fresh red thai chillies, seeded, chopped finely

2 cloves garlic, crushed

2 teaspoons grated fresh ginger

2 eggs, beaten lightly

5 green onions, sliced thinly

160g bean sprouts, tips trimmed

1 tablespoon light soy sauce

1 teaspoon thick soy sauce

¼ cup (60ml) dark soy sauce

¼ teaspoon sesame oil

1 teaspoon brown sugar

1 Cut noodle sheets into 2cm strips; place in large bowl. Cover with warm water; gently separate noodles with hands. Stand noodles 1 minute; drain.

2 Shell and devein prawns, leaving tails intact; halve prawns crossways.

3 Heat 1 tablespoon of the peanut oil in heated large wok or frying pan; stir-fry chicken, chilli, garlic and ginger about 2 minutes or until chicken is tender. Remove from wok; cover.

4 Heat half of the remaining peanut oil in wok; stir-fry prawns about 2 minutes or until prawns change colour. Remove from wok; cover.

5 Stir-fry egg, onion and sprouts in wok until egg is just set. Remove from wok; cover.

6 Place remaining peanut oil in wok; stir-fry noodles and combined remaining ingredients 1 minute. Return chicken, prawns and egg mixture to wok; stir-fry until heated through.

serves 6

per serving 15.2g fat; 1680kJ

roti canai

PREPARATION TIME 40 MINUTES (plus standing time) ■ COOKING TIME 25 MINUTES

3 cups (450g) plain flour

1 teaspoon sugar

1 egg

**¾ cup (180ml) warm
    water, approximately**

100g ghee, melted, approximately

1 Combine flour and sugar in large bowl; stir in egg and enough of the water to mix to a soft dough. Turn dough onto lightly floured surface; knead about 10 minutes or until smooth and elastic. Cover dough with plastic wrap; stand 2 hours.

2 Divide dough into 12 portions. Roll out one portion on lightly floured surface to form 18cm circle. Brush circle with a little of the ghee. Roll dough up tightly like a swiss roll, then roll up both ends so that they meet in the centre. Repeat with remaining dough portions. While working with dough, keep other portions covered with plastic wrap to prevent them from drying out. If making ahead, brush rolls with a little of the ghee; cover with plastic wrap.

3 Roll out rolls on lightly floured surface into 17cm circles. Cook roti over high heat in heavy-based pan greased with ghee, until puffed and browned lightly on both sides.

makes 12

per serving 9.2g fat; 885kJ

beef
rendang

PREPARATION TIME 20 MINUTES ■ COOKING TIME 1 HOUR 45 MINUTES

2 medium red onions (340g), chopped finely

4 cloves garlic, peeled

4 fresh red thai chillies

1 tablespoon grated fresh ginger

1 tablespoon finely chopped fresh lemon grass

1 teaspoon ground turmeric

2 teaspoons ground coriander

1$\frac{2}{3}$ cups (410ml) coconut milk

1kg beef blade steak, cut into 3cm cubes

1 cinnamon stick

1 tablespoon thick tamarind concentrate

8 curry leaves

1 teaspoon sugar

1 Blend or process onion, garlic, chillies, ginger, lemon grass, turmeric and coriander with $\frac{1}{3}$ cup (80ml) of the coconut milk until smooth.

2 Combine beef, coconut mixture, remaining coconut milk, cinnamon stick, tamarind concentrate and curry leaves in large saucepan; simmer, uncovered, about 1$\frac{1}{2}$ hours, stirring occasionally, or until beef is tender.

3 Add sugar; cook, stirring, about 15 minutes or until beef is dark and most of the sauce has evaporated.

serves 4

per serving 31.1g fat; 2297kJ
tips Recipe best made a day ahead and refrigerated, covered; can be frozen for up to 3 months.
Beef round steak, skirt steak and gravy beef can be substituted for the blade steak, if preferred.

chicken satay
noodles

PREPARATION TIME 15 MINUTES ■ COOKING TIME 10 MINUTES

2 teaspoons ground coriander

2 teaspoons ground cumin

2 teaspoons ground turmeric

700g chicken thigh fillets, chopped coarsely

250g hokkien noodles

6 green onions

150g fresh baby corn

2 tablespoons peanut oil

1 large carrot (180g), sliced thinly

2 tablespoons finely chopped fresh coriander

satay sauce

½ cup (130g) crunchy peanut butter

½ cup (125ml) coconut cream

½ cup (125ml) chicken stock

2 tablespoons sweet chilli sauce

2 tablespoons soy sauce

1 tablespoon brown sugar

1 tablespoon lime juice

1 Combine ground coriander, cumin and turmeric in medium bowl. Add chicken; mix well to coat with spices. *[Can be made a day ahead to this stage and refrigerated, covered, or frozen for up to a month.]*

2 Rinse noodles under hot running water; drain. Transfer to large bowl; separate noodles with fork.

3 Chop onions and corn diagonally into 4cm pieces.

4 Heat half of the oil in heated large wok or frying pan; stir-fry chicken mixture, in batches, until browned.

5 Heat remaining oil in wok; stir-fry corn and carrot until just tender. Return chicken to wok with noodles, onion and satay sauce; stir-fry until heated through. Sprinkle with fresh coriander.

satay sauce Combine ingredients in medium jug; whisk until combined.

serves 4

per serving 45.6g fat; 2753kJ

tip Bottled satay sauce can be substituted for the satay sauce, and rice or egg noodles can be substituted for hokkien noodles, if preferred.

fish curry with lemon grass

PREPARATION TIME 15 MINUTES ■ COOKING TIME 25 MINUTES

1kg boneless white fish fillets

¼ cup (60ml) peanut oil

3 large brown onions (600g), sliced thickly

4 cloves garlic, crushed

2 tablespoons finely chopped fresh ginger

1 teaspoon ground turmeric

1 tablespoon finely chopped fresh lemon grass

2 tablespoons brown vinegar

1 tablespoon fish sauce

½ cup (125ml) water

2 medium tomatoes (380g), chopped coarsely

2 tablespoons coarsely chopped fresh coriander

1 Cut fish into strips. Heat oil in large frying pan; cook fish, stirring, over medium heat about 1 minute or until fish is cooked slightly. Remove from heat; keep warm.

2 Add onion and garlic to pan; stir over medium heat about 5 minutes or until onion is soft.

3 Stir in ginger, turmeric, lemon grass, vinegar and sauce; bring to a boil. Reduce heat; simmer, uncovered, 3 minutes.

4 Stir in fish and the water; bring to a boil. Reduce heat; simmer, uncovered, about 5 minutes or until fish is tender. Stir in tomato; cook over low heat until mixture is heated through. Stir in coriander.

serves 4

per serving 21.7g fat; 1918kJ

beef and pork satays

PREPARATION TIME 25 MINUTES (plus marinating time) ■ COOKING TIME 20 MINUTES

500g piece beef fillet
500g piece pork fillet
4 cloves garlic, crushed
1 teaspoon ground cumin
1 teaspoon ground coriander
2 teaspoons ground turmeric
2 tablespoons vegetable oil

peanut sauce
8 green onions, chopped coarsely
1 cup (150g) unsalted
** roasted peanuts**
2 teaspoons vegetable oil
1 tablespoon finely chopped
** fresh lemon grass**
1 clove garlic, crushed
1 teaspoon grated fresh ginger
1 teaspoon sambal oelek
1 teaspoon ground cumin
1 teaspoon ground coriander
½ teaspoon ground turmeric
1 cup (250ml) chicken stock
1 cup (250ml) coconut milk
2 teaspoons lemon juice

1 Cut beef and pork into 8cm-long strips, about 1.5cm thick; thread evenly onto 18 bamboo skewers.

2 Place skewers on oven trays; brush with combined garlic, spices and half of the oil. Cover; refrigerate 3 hours or until required. *[Can be made a day ahead to this stage, or frozen for up to 3 months.]*

3 Heat remaining oil in large frying pan, cook skewers, in batches, until well browned and tender. Serve with peanut sauce.

peanut sauce Blend or process onion and nuts until chopped finely. Heat oil in medium saucepan; cook peanut mixture, lemon grass, garlic, ginger, sambal oelek and spices, stirring, 2 minutes. Stir in stock and coconut milk; simmer, uncovered, about 5 minutes or until thickened slightly. Stir in juice.

serves 6

per serving 34.5g fat; 2117kJ
tip Soak bamboo skewers in water several hours or overnight to prevent them from burning.

hot tomato chutney

PREPARATION TIME 10 MINUTES
COOKING TIME 15 MINUTES

- **1 tablespoon peanut oil**
- **1/2 teaspoon black mustard seeds**
- **2 cloves garlic, chopped finely**
- **1 fresh red thai chilli, chopped finely**
- **1 teaspoon finely chopped fresh ginger**
- **1 cinnamon stick**
- **1 teaspoon ground cumin**
- **1 teaspoon ground turmeric**
- **410g canned tomatoes**
- **1 teaspoon brown sugar**
- **6 dried curry leaves**

1 Heat oil in small saucepan; stir in seeds. Cover; cook over medium heat until seeds begin to pop. Stir in garlic, chilli, ginger and cinnamon; stir over medium heat about 3 minutes or until garlic is golden brown.

2 Stir in cumin and turmeric; stir over medium heat 2 minutes. Stir in undrained crushed tomatoes, sugar and curry leaves; bring to a boil. Reduce heat; simmer, uncovered, about 5 minutes or until chutney is thick. Discard cinnamon. Pour chutney into hot sterilised jar; seal while hot.

makes 1 cup

per tablespoon 1.7g fat; 94kJ
tip Recipe can be made a week ahead and refrigerated.

fresh coriander coconut chutney

PREPARATION TIME 10 MINUTES

- **1/3 cup (80ml) boiling water**
- **1/3 cup (25g) shredded coconut**
- **2 cups loosely packed fresh coriander**
- **4 cloves garlic, chopped finely**
- **1 small brown onion (80g), chopped finely**
- **1 1/2 teaspoons garam masala**
- **1/4 cup (60ml) lemon juice**
- **2 tablespoons lime juice**
- **1 small fresh red chilli, chopped finely**

1 Pour the water over coconut in small heatproof bowl. Cover; stand about 5 minutes or until liquid is absorbed.

2 Blend or process coconut mixture, coriander, garlic, onion, garam masala and juices until well combined. Return mixture to bowl; stir in chilli.

makes 1 1/2 cups

per tablespoon 1g fat; 56kJ
tip Recipe can be made a day ahead and refrigerated, covered.

ginger and lemon grass sauce

PREPARATION TIME 10 MINUTES
COOKING TIME 10 MINUTES

½ cup (125ml) white vinegar
½ cup (110g) sugar
¼ cup (60ml) water
1 stalk fresh lemon grass, sliced thinly
2cm piece fresh ginger, shredded finely
2 tablespoons fish sauce

1 Combine vinegar, sugar, the water, lemon grass and ginger in small saucepan; cook, stirring, without boiling, until sugar dissolves. Bring to a boil; reduce heat. Simmer, uncovered, 7 minutes or until sauce thickens slightly. Stir in fish sauce; cool.

makes ½ cup

per ½ cup 0.2g fat; 1944kJ
tip Recipe can be made 2 days ahead and refrigerated, covered.

mango sambal

PREPARATION TIME 10 MINUTES
COOKING TIME 5 MINUTES

1 teaspoon shrimp paste
1 large mango (600g), peeled
1 fresh red thai chilli, chopped finely
1 teaspoon sugar
½ teaspoon soy sauce

1 Cook paste in dry, non-stick small saucepan until dry and crumbly.

2 Cut mango into 1cm cubes. Combine paste, mango, chilli, sugar and sauce in medium bowl; mix well.

makes 1½ cups

per ½ cup 0.4g fat; 371kJ
tip Recipe can be made a day ahead and refrigerated, covered.

side dishes

indonesia

Lime, coconut, tamarind and lemon grass are just a few of the many flavours of Indonesia. Seafood predominates (as you'd expect in a country made up of thousands of islands) and while many of the dishes are subtle and fragrant, most Indonesian meals are livened up with tiny bowls of fiery sambal.

meatball soup

PREPARATION TIME 20 MINUTES (plus refrigeration time) ■ COOKING TIME 2 HOURS 15 MINUTES

2kg chicken bones (carcass, neck, wings, etc)

2 medium brown onions (300g), chopped coarsely

2 trimmed sticks celery (150g), chopped coarsely

2 medium carrots (250g), chopped coarsely

4 litres (16 cups) water

1 small white onion (80g), chopped finely

2 cloves garlic, crushed

500g veal mince

2 tablespoons ketjap manis

2 tablespoons soy sauce

80g bean sprouts, tips trimmed

4 green onions, sliced thinly

1 Combine bones, brown onion, celery, carrot and the water in large saucepan; bring to a boil. Reduce heat; simmer, uncovered, 2 hours. Strain through muslin-lined strainer into large bowl. Reserve stock; discard bones and vegetables. *[Can be made a day ahead to this stage and refrigerated, covered, or frozen for up to 3 months.]*

2 Using hands, combine white onion, garlic, veal, half of the ketjap manis and half of the sauce in large bowl. Roll rounded teaspoons of veal mixture into balls; place on tray. Cover; refrigerate 30 minutes. *[Can be made a day ahead to this stage and refrigerated, covered, or frozen for up to a month.]*

3 Combine remainder of ketjap manis and sauce with stock in large saucepan; bring to a boil. Add meatballs; reduce heat. Simmer, uncovered, stirring occasionally, about 10 minutes or until meatballs are cooked through.

4 Divide soup among serving bowls; top with sprouts and green onion.

serves 6

per serving 2.1g fat; 1016kJ
tip Cook meatballs in soup close to serving time, to prevent soup becoming cloudy.

tempeh vegetable baskets

PREPARATION TIME 20 MINUTES ▪ COOKING TIME 15 MINUTES (plus standing time)

4 spring roll wrappers

1 egg white

vegetable filling

1 tablespoon crunchy peanut butter

1/4 cup (60ml) soy sauce

200g tempeh, chopped coarsely

2 teaspoons vegetable oil

**1 small brown onion (80g),
   chopped finely**

1 clove garlic, crushed

**2 cups (200g) canned bamboo
   shoots, rinsed, drained**

**1 medium red capsicum (200g),
   sliced thinly**

**1/2 small chinese cabbage (200g),
   sliced thinly**

2 green onions, sliced thinly

2 tablespoons green ginger wine

1 teaspoon cornflour

1/4 cup (60ml) water

1 Wet two 30cm squares of baking paper; wrap around base and sides of two 1-cup (250ml) inverted soufflé dishes. Place dishes on oven tray.

2 Brush spring roll wrappers lightly with egg white; layer two wrappers at an angle. Place over a prepared dish; shape wrappers around dish. Repeat with remaining dish and wrappers.

3 Bake baskets in moderate oven about 8 minutes or until browned lightly. Remove baskets from dishes; add vegetable filling just before serving.

vegetable filling Combine peanut butter and 2 tablespoons of the sauce in medium bowl. Stir in tempeh; stand several hours. Heat oil in heated large wok or frying pan; add tempeh mixture. Stir-fry until browned lightly; remove from wok. Add brown onion, garlic, shoots and capsicum to wok; stir fry 1 minute. Add cabbage and green onion; stir-fry until just wilted. Stir in tempeh mixture, wine, remaining sauce and blended cornflour and water; stir until mixture boils and thickens.

serves 2

per serving 16.2g fat; 1450kJ

tip We used 20cm-square spring roll wrappers for this recipe. Baskets can be made several hours ahead; filling best cooked just before serving.

gado gado

PREPARATION TIME 1 HOUR (plus cooling time) ■ COOKING TIME 35 MINUTES

2 medium potatoes (400g), sliced thickly

2 medium carrots (240g), sliced thickly

150g green beans, chopped coarsely

600g green cabbage

vegetable oil, for deep-frying

300g firm tofu, cut into 2cm cubes

2 medium tomatoes (380g), cut into wedges

2 lebanese cucumbers (260g), sliced thickly

160g bean sprouts, tips trimmed

4 hard-boiled eggs, quartered

peanut sauce

1 cup (150g) unsalted roasted peanuts

1 tablespoon peanut oil

1 small brown onion (80g), chopped finely

1 clove garlic, crushed

3 fresh red thai chillies, seeded, chopped finely

1 tablespoon finely grated fresh galangal

1 tablespoon lime juice

1 tablespoon brown sugar

½ teaspoon shrimp paste

1 cup (250ml) coconut milk

¼ teaspoon thick tamarind concentrate

1 tablespoon ketjap manis

1 Boil, steam or microwave potato, carrot and beans, separately, until potato is cooked through and carrot and beans are just tender.

2 Meanwhile, drop cabbage leaves into large saucepan of boiling water; remove leaves and quickly plunge into cold water. Drain cabbage; slice thinly.

3 Heat oil in medium saucepan; deep-fry tofu, in batches, until browned. Drain on absorbent paper.

4 Place potato, carrot, beans, cabbage, tofu, tomato, cucumber, sprouts and egg in sections on serving plate; serve with peanut sauce.

peanut sauce Blend or process nuts until chopped coarsely. Heat oil in small saucepan; cook onion, garlic and chilli, stirring, until onion is golden brown. Add nuts and remaining ingredients. Bring to a boil; reduce heat. Simmer 5 minutes or until mixture thickens; cool 10 minutes. Pour sauce into small bowl; serve with vegetable salad.

serves 4

per serving 50.4g fat; 3083kJ

tip Gado gado translates roughly as 'mixed mixed', which helps explain the casual way Indonesians eat this salad. Each diner makes his or her personal selection from the assortment of vegetables, then mixes them together, dollops on the peanut sauce and mixes the salad again. Gado gado can be eaten cold or at room temperature.

chilli chicken
and corn soup

PREPARATION TIME 10 MINUTES ■ COOKING TIME 20 MINUTES

2 tablespoons peanut oil

340g chicken breast fillets

1 medium red onion (170g), chopped finely

1 tablespoon plain flour

1.5 litres (6 cups) chicken stock

2 cups (500ml) tomato juice

420g can corn kernels, drained

2 fresh red thai chillies, seeded, chopped finely

¼ cup loosely packed fresh coriander

1 Heat half of the oil in large saucepan. Cook chicken until cooked through; when cool enough to handle, shred into small pieces.

2 Heat remaining oil in pan; cook onion, stirring, until soft. Add flour; cook, stirring, until mixture bubbles and thickens. Gradually stir in stock and juice; cook, stirring, until mixture boils and thickens.

3 Add chicken, corn and chilli; stir over heat until soup is hot. Just before serving, stir in coriander.

serves 6

per serving 8.5g fat; 1054kJ

tip A purchased barbecued chicken can be substituted for chicken breasts, if preferred; discard skin, excess fat and all bones before shredding meat.

garlic and chilli
squid

PREPARATION TIME 20 MINUTES (plus marinating time) ■ COOKING TIME 15 MINUTES

1kg squid hoods

2 teaspoons peanut oil

1 fresh red thai chilli, sliced thinly

chilli paste

2 tablespoons peanut oil

4 cloves garlic, chopped finely

**4 fresh red thai chillies,
   chopped finely**

1 tablespoon grated fresh ginger

1 tablespoon white vinegar

1 tablespoon honey

1 Cut squid hoods in half. Score inside surface; cut into 5cm pieces. Combine squid with chilli paste in large bowl. Cover; refrigerate 3 hours or until required. *[Can be made a day ahead to this stage.]*

2 Drain squid over medium bowl; reserve marinade. Heat oil in heated large wok or frying pan; stir-fry squid, in batches, until browned and tender. Add marinade to wok; bring to a boil. Reduce heat; simmer, uncovered, until mixture forms a thick glaze. Return squid to wok; stir through glaze. Serve on shredded green cabbage, if desired; top with chilli.

chilli paste Blend or process ingredients until almost smooth.

serves 4

per serving 14.5g fat; 1358kJ

nasi goreng

PREPARATION TIME 15 MINUTES ■ COOKING TIME 20 MINUTES

10g butter

2 eggs

1 tablespoon peanut oil

1 clove garlic, crushed

1 fresh red thai chilli, chopped finely

4 green onions, chopped finely

150g chicken thigh fillets, chopped finely

150g button mushrooms, sliced thinly

150g chinese barbecued pork, sliced thinly

1 small carrot (70g), sliced thinly

16 cooked shelled medium prawns

4 cups (600g) cooked jasmine rice

6 spinach leaves, shredded finely

1 tablespoon soy sauce

1 tablespoon tomato sauce

1 teaspoon hot paprika

1 Heat butter in heated large wok or frying pan; cook eggs, on one side only, until just set. Remove from wok.

2 Heat oil in wok; cook garlic, chilli and onion, stirring, until onion is just tender. Add chicken; cook, stirring, until chicken is tender.

3 Add mushrooms, pork, carrot, prawns, rice and spinach; cook, stirring, until combined and hot. Stir in sauces and paprika. Serve topped with eggs.

serves 6

per serving 12.5g fat; 1494kJ

tip Recipe can be made a day ahead and refrigerated, covered.

carrot and cucumber
salad

PREPARATION TIME 15 MINUTES

2 medium carrots (240g)

1 telegraph cucumber (400g), sliced thinly

240g mung bean sprouts, tips trimmed

1 tablespoon finely chopped fresh coriander

peanut dressing

⅓ cup (85g) smooth peanut butter

1 clove garlic, crushed

1 teaspoon sambal oelek

1 tablespoon soy sauce

½ cup (125ml) coconut milk

2 tablespoons hot water

1 Using vegetable peeler, shave long, thin strips from carrots. Gently toss carrot with remaining salad ingredients in large bowl; drizzle with peanut dressing.

peanut dressing Combine peanut butter, garlic, sambal oelek, sauce and coconut milk in small bowl. Just before serving, stir in the hot water.

serves 4

per serving 17.5g fat; 968kJ

tip Salad and peanut dressing can be made 2 days ahead and refrigerated, covered.

caramelised chicken
noodle salad

PREPARATION TIME 20 MINUTES (plus standing time) ■ COOKING TIME 20 MINUTES

1/4 cup (65g) finely chopped palm sugar

1 clove garlic, crushed

1 tablespoon lime juice

1 teaspoon fish sauce

2 teaspoons sambal oelek

750g chicken tenderloins

6 green onions

1 large carrot (180g)

2 small green capsicums (300g)

420g fresh egg noodles

sweet chilli dressing

2 tablespoons peanut oil

2 tablespoons lime juice

2 tablespoons sweet chilli sauce

1 tablespoon fish sauce

1 Cook sugar, garlic, juice, sauce and sambal oelek in large saucepan, stirring, over low heat until sugar dissolves. Simmer, uncovered, about 3 minutes or until mixture starts to caramelise.

2 Add chicken to pan; cook over low heat, uncovered, until chicken is caramelised and cooked through, turning occasionally. Remove from pan; cool 10 minutes. Slice thinly.

3 Meanwhile, cut onions into 5cm lengths; cut lengths into thin strips. Cut carrot into matchstick-sized pieces. Quarter capsicums; remove seeds and membranes. Cut capsicum into thin strips. Boil, steam or microwave carrot and capsicum, separately, until just tender; drain.

4 Place noodles in large heatproof bowl; cover with boiling water. Stand 5 minutes; drain.

5 Combine noodles, chicken, onion, carrot and capsicum in large bowl with sweet chilli dressing.

sweet chilli dressing Combine ingredients in screw-top jar; shake well.

serves 4

per serving 18.5g fat; 2319kJ

tip 1/4 cup (50g) brown sugar can be substituted for the palm sugar, if preferred.

eggplant and shrimp
sambal

PREPARATION TIME 15 MINUTES ■ COOKING TIME 20 MINUTES

⅓ cup (40g) dried shrimps
1 medium brown onion (150g), chopped finely
2 green onions, chopped finely
2 cloves garlic, crushed
2 teaspoons chilli powder
2 teaspoons white vinegar
2 teaspoons sugar
¼ cup (60ml) water
1 tablespoon vegetable oil
2 teaspoons sesame oil
2 medium eggplants (600g)
vegetable oil, for deep-frying

1 Place shrimps in small heatproof bowl; cover with boiling water. Stand about 10 minutes or until soft; drain. Blend or process shrimps, brown onion, green onion, garlic, chilli, vinegar, sugar and the water until chopped finely.

2 Heat vegetable oil and sesame oil in small frying pan; add shrimp mixture. Cook, stirring, about 2 minutes or until fragrant.

3 Cut eggplants into 1cm-thick slices; heat oil in large saucepan. Deep-fry eggplant, in batches, until browned lightly; drain on absorbent paper. Top warm eggplant slices with shrimp mixture.

serves 8

per serving 7.8g fat; 412kJ

pipis
stir-fried in coconut milk

PREPARATION TIME 15 MINUTES (plus standing time) ■ COOKING TIME 10 MINUTES

1 tablespoon peanut oil

1 medium brown onion (150g), chopped coarsely

1 tablespoon grated fresh ginger

2 cloves garlic, crushed

1 tablespoon finely chopped fresh lemon grass

2 teaspoons ground cumin

2 teaspoons ground coriander

1 teaspoon ground turmeric

1kg pipis, prepared

2 tablespoons lime juice

2 teaspoons fish sauce

1²/₃ cups (410ml) coconut milk

2 teaspoons brown sugar

500g choy sum, chopped coarsely

2 tablespoons fresh coriander

1 Heat oil in heated large wok or frying pan; stir-fry onion, ginger, garlic, lemon grass and spices until fragrant.

2 Add rinsed and drained pipis, juice, sauce, coconut milk and sugar; stir-fry until pipis open, discard any that do not open.

3 Add choy sum; stir-fry until leaves are just wilted. Serve sprinkled with coriander.

serves 4

per serving 9.6g fat; 643kJ

tip Clams or mussels can be substituted for pipis, if preferred.

potatoes
and spinach

PREPARATION TIME 10 MINUTES ■ COOKING TIME 20 MINUTES

40g ghee

2 teaspoons grated fresh ginger

1 teaspoon ground turmeric

1 teaspoon garam masala

1 teaspoon chilli powder

4 medium potatoes (800g), unpeeled, chopped coarsely

1 cup (250ml) water

650g spinach

1 Heat ghee in heated large wok or frying pan; cook ginger, turmeric, garam masala and chilli, stirring, until fragrant. Add potato, cook, stirring, 1 minute.

2 Add the water; simmer, covered, about 15 minutes or until potato is tender.

3 Stir in spinach; cook, covered, further 2 minutes.

serves 4

per serving 10.8g fat; 1035kJ

lamb curry
with coconut cream

PREPARATION TIME 15 MINUTES (plus standing time) ■ COOKING TIME 1 HOUR

1kg lamb fillets, chopped coarsely
2 tablespoons drained canned green peppercorns, crushed
plain flour
2 tablespoons olive oil
60g ghee
2 green onions, chopped finely
2 cloves garlic, crushed
2 tablespoons finely chopped fresh lemon grass
2 teaspoons coarsely chopped fresh coriander
1 teaspoon grated fresh ginger
1/4 teaspoon ground coriander
1/4 teaspoon ground cumin
1/4 teaspoon ground nutmeg
1 teaspoon grated lemon rind
2 fresh green thai chillies, chopped finely
1²/₃ cups (410ml) coconut cream
2 teaspoons sugar
1 teaspoon fish sauce
²/₃ cup (100g) unsalted roasted peanuts, chopped coarsely

1 Combine lamb and peppercorns in large bowl; stand 30 minutes. Toss lamb in flour; shake off excess.

2 Heat oil in large saucepan; cook lamb, in batches, stirring, over high heat until lamb is well browned all over. Drain on absorbent paper; discard oil in pan.

3 Melt ghee in pan; cook onion, garlic, lemon grass, fresh coriander, ginger, spices, rind and chilli, stirring over medium heat about 3 minutes or until onion and chilli are soft. Blend or process mixture until smooth.

4 Return lamb to pan; stir in spice mixture and coconut cream. Cook, covered, over low heat about 45 minutes or until lamb is tender. Stir in remaining ingredients. Reheat mixture without boiling.

serves 6

per serving 43.8g fat; 2456kJ
tip Recipe best made a day ahead and refrigerated, covered. Can be frozen for up to 3 months.

lemon grass
beef satay

PREPARATION TIME 15 MINUTES (plus marinating time ■ COOKING TIME 20 MINUTES

3/4 cup (180ml) coconut cream

1 teaspoon crunchy peanut butter

2 teaspoons sambal oelek

2 tablespoons coarsely chopped fresh lemon grass

2 cloves garlic, crushed

1 teaspoon ground coriander

1 teaspoon ground turmeric

750g beef rump steak, cut into 2cm cubes

1 Combine coconut cream, peanut butter, sambal oelek, lemon grass, garlic, coriander and turmeric in large bowl. Add beef to marinade; mix well. Cover; refrigerate several hours or until required. *[Can be made a day ahead to this stage or frozen for up to 3 months.]*

2 Remove beef from marinade; thread onto 12 bamboo skewers. Grill or barbecue skewers until beef is tender, brushing with remaining marinade during cooking.

makes 12

per serving 6.7g fat; 502kJ

tip Soak bamboo skewers in water at least 1 hour before using.

mee goreng

PREPARATION TIME 25 MINUTES ■ COOKING TIME 30 MINUTES

500g fresh wheat noodles

vegetable oil, for deep-frying

**1 small white onion (80g),
     sliced thinly**

2 tablespoons raw peanuts

2 tablespoons peanut oil

500g pork fillets, sliced thinly

5 cloves garlic, crushed

2 tablespoons grated fresh ginger

**3 fresh red thai chillies, seeded,
     chopped finely**

**10 fresh water chestnuts,
     sliced thinly**

18 snake beans (180g), sliced thickly

**2 trimmed sticks celery (150g),
     chopped finely**

2 baby bok choy, chopped coarsely

2 green onions, chopped coarsely

1/3 cup (80ml) ketjap manis

2 tablespoons sweet chilli sauce

**1 tablespoon thick
     tamarind concentrate**

1/3 cup (80ml) vegetable stock

1 teaspoon sesame oil

1 Cook noodles in large saucepan of boiling water, uncovered, until just tender; drain.

2 Heat vegetable oil in small saucepan. Deep-fry white onion until browned; drain on absorbent paper. Deep-fry peanuts until browned lightly; drain on absorbent paper. Blend or process onion and peanuts until chopped finely.

3 Heat half of the peanut oil in heated large wok or frying pan; stir-fry pork until browned and cooked as desired. Remove pork; cover to keep warm.

4 Heat remaining peanut oil in wok; stir-fry garlic, ginger and chilli until fragrant. Add water chestnuts and vegetables; stir-fry 2 minutes.

5 Return pork to pan with noodles, ketjap manis, sauce, tamarind, stock and sesame oil; stir-fry until heated through. Serve sprinkled with onion and peanut mixture.

serves 4

per serving 19.5g fat; 2090kJ
tip Recipe best made just before serving.

red mullet
with peppercorns and lime

PREPARATION TIME 10 MINUTES (plus marinating time) ■ COOKING TIME 10 MINUTES

4 medium red mullet (1kg)
2 medium limes (160g)
2 tablespoons canned green peppercorns, drained, crushed
1 tablespoon coriander seeds
1 clove garlic, crushed
1 medium red onion (170g), sliced thinly
⅔ cup (160ml) lime juice
⅓ cup (80ml) oyster sauce

1 Score each fish three times on both sides. Using vegetable peeler, peel rind thinly from limes; cut rind into thin strips. Rub fish with combined rind, peppercorns, seeds and garlic. Place fish in shallow dish; top with onion, juice and sauce. Cover; refrigerate 3 hours, turning once.

2 Remove fish from marinade; reserve marinade. Cook fish in heated oiled frying pan until cooked as desired, turning once during cooking. Add reserved marinade to pan; bring to a boil. Serve over fish.

serves 4

per serving 6.2g fat; 732kJ

almond chicken
and noodles

PREPARATION TIME 10 MINUTES (plus marinating time) ■ COOKING TIME 10 MINUTES

700g chicken breast fillets, sliced thickly

2 cloves garlic, crushed

¼ cup (60ml) hoisin sauce

¼ cup (60ml) ketjap manis

2 tablespoons peanut oil

½ cup (80g) blanched almonds

4 green onions, sliced thinly

1 medium brown onion (150g), sliced thinly

420g fresh egg noodles

200g choy sum, chopped coarsely

1 cup (250ml) chicken stock

1 Combine chicken, garlic, 2 tablespoons of the sauce and 1 tablespoon of the ketjap manis in medium bowl. Cover; refrigerate 3 hours or until required. *[Can be made a day ahead to this stage or frozen for up to 3 months.]*

2 Heat 2 teaspoons of the oil in heated large wok or frying pan; stir-fry almonds until browned. Remove from wok.

3 Heat remaining oil in wok; stir-fry chicken mixture, green onion and brown onion, in batches, until chicken is browned.

4 Place noodles in large heatproof bowl; cover with boiling water. Stand 5 minutes or until just tender; drain.

5 Return chicken mixture to wok with almonds, noodles, choy sum, stock and remaining sauce and ketjap manis; stir-fry until choy sum just wilts.

serves 4

per serving 29.4g fat; 2397kJ

satay beef salad

PREPARATION TIME 15 MINUTES (plus standing time) ■ COOKING TIME 25 MINUTES

750g piece beef eye fillet

2 medium carrots (240g)

240g bean sprouts, tips trimmed

100g snow pea sprouts

**1 medium red onion (170g),
   sliced thinly**

1/4 cup lightly packed fresh coriander

**1/3 cup (50g) coarsely chopped
   unsalted roasted peanuts**

satay sauce

2 tablespoons brown sugar

**2 tablespoons coarsely chopped
   fresh coriander**

1/4 cup (60ml) sweet chilli sauce

1/2 cup (130g) crunchy peanut butter

2 cloves garlic, crushed

1 cup (250ml) coconut milk

3/4 cup (180ml) water

1 Cook beef on heated oiled grill plate (or grill or barbecue) about 20 minutes or until browned all over and cooked as desired. Stand beef 10 minutes before cutting into thin slices.

2 Using vegetable peeler, shave long, thin strips from carrots. Combine carrot, beef, sprouts and onion in large bowl. Drizzle with satay sauce; sprinkle with coriander and nuts.

satay sauce Combine ingredients in small saucepan. Simmer, stirring, about 4 minutes or until sauce thickens; cool 5 minutes.

serves 6

per serving 30.8g fat; 2118kJ

prawn stir-fry
with tamarind

PREPARATION TIME 20 MINUTES ■ COOKING TIME 15 MINUTES

1kg uncooked king prawns, shelled

2 tablespoons vegetable oil

1 clove garlic, crushed

2 teaspoons grated fresh ginger

2 tablespoons finely chopped fresh lemon grass

4 green onions, chopped finely

1 medium red capsicum (200g), sliced thinly

2 tablespoons thick tamarind concentrate

½ cup (125ml) chicken stock

2 teaspoons cornflour

1 tablespoon water

1 Cut almost through backs of prawns; remove dark veins. Gently press prawns open along cut side with knife.

2 Heat oil in heated large wok or frying pan; stir-fry garlic, ginger, lemon grass and onion over high heat about 2 minutes or until onion is soft. Add capsicum and prawns; stir-fry over high heat about 2 minutes or until prawns just change colour.

3 Stir in combined tamarind and stock; stir-fry over high heat 1 minute. Blend cornflour with the water; stir into wok. Stir over high heat until sauce boils and thickens slightly. Serve over hot noodles, if desired.

serves 4

per serving 10.1g fat; 909kJ

stir-fried prawns
and noodles

PREPARATION TIME 15 MINUTES ■ COOKING TIME 10 MINUTES

500g medium uncooked prawns

200g dried rice noodles

1 clove garlic, crushed

2 tablespoons soy sauce

2 tablespoons fish sauce

1 teaspoon sambal oelek

80g bean sprouts, tips trimmed

¼ cup fresh coriander

1 Shell and devein prawns, leaving tails intact.

2 Place noodles in large heatproof bowl; cover with boiling water. Stand until just tender; drain. Cover to keep warm.

3 Stir-fry prawns and garlic in heated oiled large wok or frying pan until prawns just change colour. Add noodles, sauces and sambal oelek; gently stir-fry until hot. Stir in sprouts and coriander.

serves 4

per serving 1g fat; 806kJ

crisp salmon
with lemon grass paste

PREPARATION TIME 15 MINUTES ■ COOKING TIME 7 MINUTES

¼ cup (35g) unsalted
  roasted peanuts

2 fresh red thai chillies, seeded,
  chopped coarsely

1 stalk fresh lemon grass,
  chopped coarsely

½ cup tightly packed fresh coriander

⅓ cup (80ml) peanut oil

1 tablespoon lemon juice

vegetable oil, for shallow-frying

6 salmon cutlets (1kg)

1 Blend or process nuts, chilli, lemon grass, coriander, peanut oil and juice until mixture forms a paste. Cover paste; refrigerate until required.

2 Heat enough vegetable oil to cover base of large frying pan; shallow-fry fish on both sides, uncovered, until cooked as desired. Drain on absorbent paper.

3 Serve fish with paste; accompany with boiled potatoes and crisp salad, if desired.

serves 6

per serving 39.4g fat; 2010kJ

deep-fried tofu
with peanut sauce

PREPARATION TIME 20 MINUTES (plus standing time) ■ COOKING TIME 20 MINUTES

600g firm tofu, drained
vegetable oil, for deep-frying

peanut sauce
1 fresh coriander root, chopped finely
1 fresh red thai chilli, seeded, chopped finely
2 cloves garlic, crushed
1 tablespoon sugar
2 tablespoons rice vinegar
1/3 cup (90g) crunchy peanut butter
1/2 cup (125ml) coconut milk

1 Wrap tofu in three sheets of absorbent paper, weigh down with plate; stand 4 hours.

2 Cut tofu into 2cm cubes. Heat oil in large wok or frying pan. Deep-fry tofu, in batches, until well browned; drain on absorbent paper. Serve hot with warm peanut sauce; sprinkle with fresh coriander and chilli, if desired.

peanut sauce Combine coriander root, chilli, garlic, sugar and vinegar in small saucepan; stir over heat until sugar dissolves. Stir in peanut butter and coconut milk, stir until just hot. *[Can be made 3 days ahead and refrigerated, covered.]*

serves 6

per serving 25g fat; 1343kJ

peanut-crusted
lemon grass chicken

PREPARATION TIME 20 MINUTES (plus marinating time) ■ COOKING TIME 15 MINUTES

**700g chicken breast fillets,
  sliced thinly**

**4 fresh red thai chillies, seeded,
  chopped finely**

2 tablespoons grated fresh ginger

4 cloves garlic, crushed

6 kaffir lime leaves, torn

400g sugar snap peas

¼ cup (60ml) peanut oil

**2 medium red onions (340g),
  sliced thinly**

**1 cup (150g) plain
  flour, approximately**

2 eggs, beaten lightly

**2 cups (300g) raw peanuts,
  chopped finely**

**½ cup finely chopped fresh
  lemon grass**

¼ cup (60ml) chicken stock

2 tablespoons sweet chilli sauce

1 Combine chicken, chilli, ginger, garlic and lime leaves in large bowl. Cover; refrigerate 3 hours or until required. *[Can be made a day ahead or frozen for up to a month.]*

2 Boil, steam or microwave peas until just tender; drain.

3 Heat 1 tablespoon of the oil in heated large wok or frying pan; stir-fry onion, in batches, until just browned.

4 Dip chicken in flour; shake off excess. Dip chicken in egg then, using hand, press on combined nuts and lemon grass.

5 Heat remaining oil in wok; stir-fry chicken, in batches, until browned and cooked through. Drain chicken on absorbent paper; cover to keep warm. Wipe wok clean with absorbent paper.

6 Return onion to wok with combined stock and sauce. Stir-fry until sauce boils; add peas. Serve onion mixture with chicken.

serves 6

per serving 41.6g fat; 2835kJ

seafood kebabs
with lime and coconut

PREPARATION TIME 20 MINUTES (plus marinating time) ■ COOKING TIME 20 MINUTES

500g piece tuna

500g piece salmon

500g piece swordfish

1/3 cup (90g) finely chopped palm sugar

1²/3 cup (410ml) coconut cream

2 tablespoons grated kaffir lime rind

1/4 cup (60ml) kaffir lime juice

2 fresh red thai chillies, seeded, chopped finely

1 Remove any skin from fish; cut each fish into 4cm pieces. Place sugar and coconut cream in small saucepan. Stir over low heat, without boiling, until sugar dissolves; cool. Stir in rind, juice, chilli and fish. Cover; refrigerate 3 hours or until required. *[Can be made a day ahead to this stage or frozen for up to a month.]*

2 Drain fish over small saucepan; reserve marinade. Thread a mixture of fish pieces onto 12 skewers; cook on heated oiled grill plate (or grill or barbecue), uncovered, until browned lightly and just cooked through. Simmer marinade, uncovered, 1 minute or until thickened slightly; serve with kebabs.

makes 12

per serving 13.2g fat; 991kJ

tip Soak bamboo skewers in water about 1 hour to prevent them scorching.

laksa paste

PREPARATION TIME 10 MINUTES
COOKING TIME 5 MINUTES

- 2 teaspoons shrimp paste
- 1 large brown onion (200g), chopped finely
- 4 cloves garlic, chopped finely
- 1 teaspoon finely grated lime rind
- 1 teaspoon ground turmeric
- 1 tablespoon coarsely chopped fresh lemon grass
- 1 tablespoon finely grated fresh ginger
- 1 tablespoon coarsely chopped vietnamese mint
- 3 fresh red thai chillies
- 8 candlenuts (20g)
- 2 teaspoons ground coriander
- 2 tablespoons coarsely chopped fresh coriander
- ¾ cup (180ml) vegetable oil

1 Cook paste in small non-stick saucepan until fragrant.

2 Blend or process paste, onion, garlic, rind, turmeric, lemon grass, ginger, mint, chillies, candlenuts, ground coriander, fresh coriander and ½ cup of the oil until mixture forms a paste.

3 Spoon into hot sterilised jars. Add remaining oil, leaving 1cm space between oil and top of jar; seal jar.

makes 1 cup (250ml)

per tablespoon 15.2g fat; 601kJ
tip Best made a day ahead. Paste can be made a month ahead and refrigerated or frozen for up to 3 months.

red curry paste

PREPARATION TIME 15 MINUTES

- 1 small red onion (100g), chopped coarsely
- 3 cloves garlic, halved
- 2 tablespoons coarsely chopped fresh lemon grass
- 3 teaspoons coarsely chopped fresh coriander root
- 2 teaspoons dried chilli flakes
- 1 teaspoon galangal powder
- 1 teaspoon finely grated lime rind
- ½ teaspoon shrimp paste
- 1 dried kaffir lime leaf
- 3 teaspoons hot paprika
- ½ teaspoon ground turmeric
- ½ teaspoon cumin seeds
- 3 teaspoons peanut oil

1 Blend or process ingredients until smooth. Spoon into hot sterilised jar; seal while hot.

makes ¾ cup

per tablespoon 5.3g fat; 289kJ
tip Recipe can be made a month ahead and refrigerated or frozen for up to 3 months.

green curry paste

PREPARATION TIME 15 MINUTES

- **3 fresh green thai chillies, seeded, sliced thickly**
- **3 green onions, chopped coarsely**
- **2 cloves garlic, halved**
- **¼ cup coarsely chopped fresh coriander**
- **¼ cup coarsely chopped fresh lemon grass**
- **¼ cup (60ml) peanut oil**
- **2 tablespoons water**
- **1 teaspoon shrimp paste**
- **½ teaspoon ground cumin**
- **225g can bamboo shoots, drained, sliced thickly**

1 Blend or process ingredients until smooth. Spoon into hot sterilised jar; seal while hot.

makes ¾ cup

per tablespoon 6.9g fat; 277kJ
tip Recipe can be made a month ahead and refrigerated or frozen for up to 3 months.

garam masala

PREPARATION TIME 10 MINUTES
COOKING TIME 2 MINUTES

- **2 tablespoons cumin seeds**
- **1 tablespoon black peppercorns**
- **2 teaspoons cloves**
- **2 tablespoons coriander seeds**
- **2 teaspoons caraway seeds**
- **1½ teaspoons cardamom seeds**
- **1 cinnamon stick**
- **½ fresh nutmeg, cracked**

1 Combine ingredients in small saucepan; stir over medium heat about 2 minutes or until fragrant. Blend or process mixture until fine.

makes ½ cup

per tablespoon 1.7g fat; 152kJ
tip Recipe can be made 2 months ahead and refrigerated in airtight container.

curry pastes

india

Indian cooking is distinguished by its use of spices. Blended carefully
and with almost infinite variety, they flavour curry, kofta, dhal and
most other dishes. While Indian food can be hot or mild, depending on
your preference, the meat-based dishes of northern India tend mainly to be
milder than the fiery food from the south, which is most often vegetarian.

lentil dhal with chapatis

PREPARATION TIME 45 MINUTES (plus standing time) ■ COOKING TIME 1 HOUR

2¹/₂ cups (500g) brown lentils

30g butter

2 medium brown onions (300g), chopped finely

2 fresh red thai chillies, chopped finely

1 teaspoon ground cumin

1 teaspoon ground coriander

¹/₂ teaspoon garam masala

¹/₂ teaspoon ground cardamom

1.5 litres (6 cups) vegetable stock

1 teaspoon ground turmeric

chapatis

3 cups (600g) plain flour

1 cup (160g) wholemeal plain flour

125g butter

2 teaspoons cumin seeds

1¹/₃ cups (330ml) hot water

50g ghee

1 Cover lentils with water in large bowl; stand, covered, overnight.

2 Heat butter in large saucepan; cook onion, chilli and spices, stirring, over medium heat about 2 minutes or until onion is just soft.

3 Stir in drained lentils, stock and turmeric; bring to a boil. Reduce heat; simmer, uncovered, about 50 minutes or until mixture is thick. *[Can be made a day ahead and refrigerated, covered.]*

chapatis Combine flours in large bowl. Rub in butter; stir in seeds. Gradually add the water; mix to a soft dough. Knead dough on unfloured surface until smooth and elastic; cut dough in half. Cut each half into nine even portions; knead each portion well. Roll each portion of dough into a long thin sausage. Roll up into a coil; flatten with hand. Roll coil out to a 15cm round. Heat heavy-based frying pan over medium heat; lightly grease with ghee. Cook chapatis, one at a time, pressing edge of each chapati lightly with a clean cloth during cooking to encourage it to rise. When golden brown patches appear on bottom, turn and cook other side until golden brown, pressing edge with cloth.

serves 6

per serving 33.4g fat; 3876kJ

vegetable fritters
with yogurt dip

PREPARATION TIME 20 MINUTES ■ COOKING TIME 20 MINUTES

¾ cup (110g) besan flour

¾ cup (110g) self-raising flour

2 cloves garlic, crushed

1½ teaspoons garam masala

1 teaspoon chilli powder

1 teaspoon cumin seeds

1 tablespoon coarsely chopped
 fresh coriander

1 cup (250ml) water

1 medium potato (200g),
 chopped finely

1 small eggplant (230g),
 chopped finely

1 medium zucchini (120g),
 chopped finely

250g cauliflower, chopped finely

vegetable oil, for deep-frying

yogurt dip

1 teaspoon cumin seeds

1 cup (280g) yogurt

1 fresh red thai chilli,
 chopped finely

½ teaspoon paprika

2 tablespoons finely chopped
 fresh mint

1 tablespoon finely chopped
 fresh coriander

1 Place flours in large bowl. Stir in garlic, garam masala, chilli, seeds and coriander. Make well in centre; gradually stir in the water. Mix to a batter; stir in vegetables. *[Can be made 3 hours ahead to this stage and refrigerated, covered.]*

2 Heat oil in heated large wok or frying pan; deep-fry heaped tablespoons of vegetable mixture, in batches, until golden brown; drain on absorbent paper. Serve hot with yogurt dip and lime wedges, if desired.

yogurt dip Place seeds in small frying pan, stir over medium heat about 2 minutes or until fragrant. Remove from heat; cool. Combine seeds with remaining ingredients in small bowl; mix well.

makes 45

per fritter 1.9g fat; 173kJ

butter chicken
with onion pilaf

PREPARATION TIME 30 MINUTES (plus marinating time) ■ COOKING TIME 1 HOUR 45 MINUTES

1 cup (150g) raw cashews

2 teaspoons garam masala

2 teaspoons ground coriander

3/4 teaspoon chilli powder

3 cloves garlic, chopped coarsely

2 teaspoons grated fresh ginger

2 tablespoons white vinegar

1/3 cup (80g) tomato paste

1/2 cup (140g) yogurt

1kg chicken thigh fillets, halved

80g butter

1 large brown onion (200g), chopped finely

1 cinnamon stick

4 cardamom pods, bruised

1 teaspoon paprika

400g can tomato puree

3/4 cup (180ml) chicken stock

1 cup (250ml) cream

onion pilaf

40g butter

3 large brown onions (600g), chopped finely

1 tablespoon cumin seeds

3 cups (600g) basmati rice

1.5 litres (6 cups) chicken stock

1 Stir nuts, garam masala, coriander and chilli in heated small frying pan until nuts are browned lightly.

2 Blend or process nut mixture with garlic, ginger, vinegar, paste and half of the yogurt until just smooth. Transfer mixture to large bowl; combine nut mixture, remaining yogurt and chicken. Cover; refrigerate 3 hours or until required. *[Can be made a day ahead to this stage and refrigerated, covered.]*

3 Melt butter in large saucepan; cook onion, cinnamon and cardamom, stirring, until onion is browned. Add chicken mixture; cook 10 minutes.

4 Add paprika, puree and stock; bring to a boil. Reduce heat; simmer, uncovered, 45 minutes, stirring occasionally. *[Can be made a day ahead to this stage and refrigerated, covered.]*

5 Remove and discard cinnamon and cardamom. Add cream; simmer 5 minutes. Serve with onion pilaf.

onion pilaf Melt butter in medium saucepan; cook onion and seeds, stirring, until onion is browned lightly. Add rice; cook, stirring, 1 minute. Stir in stock; bring to a boil. Reduce heat; simmer, covered tightly, about 25 minutes or until rice is just tender and liquid is absorbed. Remove from heat; fluff rice with fork. Stand, covered, 5 minutes.

serves 4

per serving 82.9g fat; 7297kJ

potato-crusted **snapper**

PREPARATION TIME 30 MINUTES ■ COOKING TIME 20 MINUTES

2 tablespoons peanut oil

1 medium brown onion (150g), chopped finely

1 tablespoon grated fresh ginger

3 cloves garlic, crushed

1 teaspoon garam masala

2 teaspoons ground turmeric

1 teaspoon ground cumin

1 teaspoon ground coriander

4 medium tomatoes (720g), chopped coarsely

4 kaffir lime leaves, torn

2 teaspoons sugar

1/2 cup (125ml) coconut cream

2 tablespoons coarsely chopped fresh coriander

4 snapper fillets (800g)

2 small potatoes (240g), sliced thinly

40g butter, melted

1/2 teaspoon ground cumin, extra

1 teaspoon ground turmeric, extra

1 Heat half of the oil in medium frying pan; cook onion, ginger and two-thirds of the garlic, stirring, until onion is soft. Stir in garam masala, turmeric, cumin and ground coriander; cook, stirring, about 2 minutes or until fragrant. Add tomato, lime leaves and sugar; cook, stirring, about 5 minutes or until tomato is just tender. Add coconut cream; simmer, uncovered, stirring occasionally, 10 minutes.

2 Just before serving, discard lime leaves; stir in fresh coriander. *[Can be made a day ahead to this stage and refrigerated, covered.]*

3 Meanwhile, heat remaining oil in large frying pan; cook fish, uncovered, about 3 minutes each side or until just cooked through. Place fish, skin-side down, on oven tray. Place potato in single layer over fish; drizzle with combined butter, extra cumin, extra turmeric and remaining garlic. Cook under heated grill about 10 minutes or until potato is crisp. Serve potato-crusted fish with warm curried tomato.

serves 4

per serving 30.5g fat; 2231kJ

tip You can use any firm-fleshed fish fillets for this recipe.

prawns
with chilli and mustard seeds

PREPARATION TIME 20 MINUTES ■ COOKING TIME 15 MINUTES

1.5kg medium uncooked prawns

1 large brown onion (200g), chopped coarsely

2 cloves garlic, chopped coarsely

2 teaspoons coarsely chopped fresh ginger

2 fresh red thai chillies, chopped coarsely

1 teaspoon ground turmeric

2 tablespoons lemon juice

2 tablespoons ghee

1 tablespoon black mustard seeds

1 teaspoon cumin seeds

1/3 cup (80ml) coconut milk

1 Shell and devein prawns, leaving tails intact.

2 Blend or process onion, garlic, ginger, chilli, turmeric and juice until smooth. Heat ghee in heated large wok or frying pan; stir-fry onion mixture about 5 minutes or until browned lightly. Add seeds; stir-fry until fragrant. Add prawns; stir-fry until prawns just change colour.

3 Add coconut milk; stir-fry until hot.

serves 4

per serving 14.6g fat; 1320kJ

lamb do piazza
with sambal

PREPARATION TIME 20 MINUTES (plus marinating time) ■ COOKING TIME 1 HOUR 20 MINUTES

5 cloves garlic, crushed

2 teaspoons grated fresh ginger

1 teaspoon cardamom seeds

1 teaspoon ground turmeric

1 teaspoon cayenne pepper

2 tablespoons water

**5 large brown onions (1kg),
sliced thickly**

1kg diced lamb

1/3 cup (80ml) vegetable oil

1 teaspoon fennel seeds

2 teaspoons fenugreek seeds

3/4 cup (210g) yogurt

**4 small tomatoes (500g),
seeded, diced**

2 cups (500ml) beef stock

2 tablespoons lime juice

**1/4 cup finely chopped
fresh coriander**

banana tamarind sambal

1 tablespoon tamarind paste

2 teaspoons sugar

1 teaspoon ground cumin

1 cup mashed banana

1 tablespoon lemon juice

1/4 cup (35g) dried currants

1 Blend or process garlic, ginger, cardamom seeds, turmeric, cayenne pepper, the water and half of the onion until pureed; transfer marinade to large non-reactive bowl. Add lamb; toss to coat with marinade. Cover; refrigerate 3 hours or until required. *[Can be made a day ahead to this stage and refrigerated, covered.]*

2 Heat oil in large frying pan; cook remaining onion until browned lightly. Remove from pan; reserve. Cook fennel seeds and fenugreek seeds in pan, stirring, 1 minute or until seeds pop. Add lamb mixture; cook, stirring, until browned all over. Add yogurt, in four batches, stirring well between additions. Add tomato and stock; bring to a boil. Reduce heat; simmer, covered, about 1 hour or until lamb is tender.

3 Stir in the reserved onion; simmer, uncovered, until heated through. *[Can be made a day ahead to this stage and refrigerated, covered.]*

4 Just before serving, stir in juice and coriander; serve with banana tamarind sambal.

banana tamarind sambal Combine ingredients in small bowl. Cover; refrigerate 30 minutes. *[Can be made a day ahead and refrigerated, covered.]*

serves 6

per serving 25.7g fat; 2160kJ
tip On average, 2 overripe large bananas make 1 cup mashed banana.

pork and snake beans
madras

PREPARATION TIME 10 MINUTES ■ COOKING TIME 20 MINUTES

**4 bacon rashers (300g),
chopped finely**

1 tablespoon peanut oil

700g pork fillets, sliced thinly

**1 large white onion (200g),
sliced thickly**

¼ cup (75g) madras curry paste

200g snake beans, chopped coarsely

½ cup (125ml) beef stock

1 tablespoon tomato paste

1 Stir-fry bacon in heated dry large wok or frying pan until crisp; drain on absorbent paper.

2 Heat oil in wok; stir-fry pork and onion, in batches, until browned.

3 Stir-fry curry paste in wok until just fragrant.

4 Add beans to wok with bacon, pork mixture, stock and paste; stir-fry, tossing until sauce boils.

serves 4

per serving 17.4g fat; 1615kJ

fish kofta

PREPARATION TIME 30 MINUTES (plus refrigeration time) ■ COOKING TIME 30 MINUTES

700g boneless white fish fillets, chopped coarsely

2 medium brown onions (300g), chopped coarsely

½ cup firmly packed fresh coriander

2 fresh red dutch chillies, chopped coarsely

1 tablespoon ghee

2 cloves garlic, crushed

2 teaspoons ground coriander

1 teaspoon ground cumin

½ teaspoon ground turmeric

2 cinnamon sticks

1 teaspoon ground fenugreek

3 medium tomatoes (570g), peeled, chopped finely

1 Place fish in large saucepan of boiling water; reduce heat immediately. Simmer, uncovered, until fish is just tender. Strain fish over large bowl; reserve 2 cups (500ml) liquid.

2 Blend or process fish with half of the onion, half of the fresh coriander and chilli until just combined.

3 Shape rounded tablespoons of mixture into egg shapes (kofta); place on tray. Refrigerate, covered, 30 minutes. *[Can be made a day ahead to this stage.]*

4 Heat half of the ghee in large non-stick frying pan; cook kofta, in batches, until browned on both sides. Drain on absorbent paper.

5 Heat remaining ghee in large saucepan; cook remaining onion, garlic and spices, stirring, until onion is browned lightly. Add tomato; cook, stirring, about 5 minutes or until tomato is very soft. Add reserved liquid; simmer, uncovered, about 10 minutes or until sauce thickens.

6 Add kofta; simmer 5 minutes or until kofta are heated through. Just before serving, stir in remaining coriander.

serves 4

per serving 10.5g fat; 1180J

tip Recipe can be made a day ahead and refrigerated, covered.

beef korma

PREPARATION TIME 20 MINUTES ■ COOKING TIME 2 HOURS

60g ghee

¼ cup (40g) blanched almonds

2 medium brown onions (300g), chopped finely

1 cup (250ml) coconut milk

2 cinnamon sticks

10 cardamom pods, crushed

4 bay leaves

3 cloves

1 tablespoon ground cumin

2 teaspoons ground coriander

1 fresh red thai chilli, chopped finely

1½ tablespoons grated fresh ginger

4 cloves garlic, crushed

1kg beef chuck steak, cut into 3cm pieces

½ cup (140g) yogurt

1 teaspoon salt

½ cup (125ml) water

1 tablespoon thick tamarind concentrate

1 Melt 20g of the ghee in medium saucepan; cook nuts and onion, stirring, until nuts are browned lightly.

2 Remove from pan; cool. Blend or process onion mixture with coconut milk until smooth.

3 Melt remaining ghee in pan; cook whole and ground spices, chilli, ginger and garlic, stirring, until fragrant. Add beef; mix well.

4 Add yogurt, 1 tablespoon at a time; cook, stirring well between additions.

5 Stir in onion mixture, salt and the water; simmer, covered, 1³/4 hours. Add tamarind concentrate; simmer, uncovered, about 15 minutes, or until beef is tender.

serves 6

per serving 30.2g fat; 1924kJ

tip Recipe can be made a day ahead and refrigerated, covered.

masala prawns

PREPARATION TIME 15 MINUTES ■ COOKING TIME 10 MINUTES

1.5kg uncooked king prawns

½ cup firmly packed fresh mint

½ cup firmly packed fresh coriander

½ cup (125ml) water

2 cloves garlic, chopped finely

2 teaspoons grated fresh ginger

1 teaspoon sambal oelek

2 teaspoons cumin seeds

1 teaspoon fennel seeds

½ teaspoon ground turmeric

¼ teaspoon ground cardamom

1 tablespoon peanut oil

1 large brown onion (200g), cut into thin wedges

150g sugar snap peas

2 tablespoons lime juice

½ cup (140g) low-fat yogurt

1 Shell and devein prawns, leaving tails intact. Blend or process mint, coriander, the water, garlic, ginger, sambal oelek, seeds, turmeric and cardamom until smooth.

2 Heat oil in large frying pan; cook onion, stirring over medium heat 3 minutes, or until soft. Add herb paste, stir over heat 1 minute.

3 Add prawns and peas, cook 4 minutes, or until just cooked through. Sprinkle with juice; serve with yogurt in separate bowl.

serves 4

per serving 7g fat; 1141kJ

sour duck curry

PREPARATION TIME 15 MINUTES ■ COOKING TIME 50 MINUTES

1.6kg duck

1 large brown onion (200g), chopped finely

1 tablespoon ground coriander

1 teaspoon ground ginger

½ teaspoon ground turmeric

½ teaspoon ground cardamom

¼ teaspoon paprika

1 teaspoon thick tamarind concentrate

2 cups (500ml) chicken stock

2 tablespoons water

1 tablespoon cornflour

1 tablespoon coarsely chopped fresh coriander

1 Cut duck into serving-sized pieces. Cook duck, in batches, in large heated frying pan until browned on both sides; drain on absorbent paper.

2 Drain fat from pan; reserve 1 tablespoon. Heat reserved fat in pan; cook onion, stirring, 1 minute. Add ground coriander, ginger, turmeric, cardamom and paprika; cook, stirring, further 2 minutes or until spices are fragrant. Stir in tamarind concentrate and stock.

3 Return duck to pan; bring to a boil. Reduce heat; simmer, uncovered, 30 minutes or until duck is tender.

4 Combine the water and cornflour in small bowl; stir into duck mixture. Stir over medium heat until sauce boils and thickens. Stir fresh coriander through just before serving. Serve with spiced pappadums, if desired.

serves 4

per serving 56.1g fat; 2652kJ

raan

PREPARATION TIME 15 MINUTES (plus marinating time) ■ COOKING TIME 1 HOUR 45 MINUTES

2 teaspoons cumin seeds

2 teaspoons coriander seeds

2 teaspoons black mustard seeds

6 cardamom pods, bruised

½ teaspoon ground cinnamon

½ teaspoon cracked black pepper

¼ teaspoon ground cloves

4 cloves garlic, crushed

1 tablespoon grated fresh ginger

¼ cup (60ml) white vinegar

2 tablespoons tomato paste

1 teaspoon sambal oelek

2kg leg of lamb

½ cup (125ml) boiling water

4 dried curry leaves, torn

10 medium potatoes (2kg), cut into 2cm dice

2 tablespoons ghee

2 teaspoons black mustard seeds, extra

2 teaspoons ground cumin

2 teaspoons ground coriander

1 Combine seeds, pods, cinnamon, pepper and cloves in heated large dry saucepan; cook, stirring, until fragrant. Blend or process cooled spice mixture until crushed; combine in small bowl with garlic, ginger, vinegar, paste and sambal oelek.

2 Trim lamb; pierce all over with sharp knife. Rub spice mixture all over lamb, pressing firmly into cuts. Place lamb in large bowl. Cover; refrigerate overnight. *[Can be made 2 days ahead to this stage and refrigerated, covered, or frozen for up to 2 months.]*

3 Pour combined water and curry leaves into large baking dish; place lamb on oven rack in dish. Cover lamb with foil; bake in moderate oven 1 hour. Remove and discard foil; bake about 30 minutes or until lamb is browned and tender.

4 Meanwhile, boil, steam or microwave potatoes until just tender; drain. Heat ghee in large flameproof casserole dish; cook remaining spices, stirring, 1 minute. Add potatoes; cook, stirring, until browned all over. Bake, uncovered, in hot oven about 15 minutes or until very crisp and well browned; serve with lamb.

serves 6

per serving 21.5g fat; 2227kJ

samosas

PREPARATION TIME 30 MINUTES (plus cooling time) ■ COOKING TIME 10 MINUTES

**5 sheets ready-rolled
  shortcrust pastry**

1 tablespoon milk

vegetable oil, for deep-frying

curried vegetable filling

2 tablespoons vegetable oil

**1 medium brown onion (150g),
  chopped finely**

1 clove garlic, crushed

2 teaspoons mild curry powder

**1 large potato (300g),
  chopped finely**

1 small carrot (70g), chopped finely

2 tablespoons frozen peas

meat filling

1 tablespoon vegetable oil

**1 small brown onion (80g),
  chopped finely**

1 clove garlic, crushed

1 teaspoon grated fresh ginger

1/4 teaspoon dried chilli flakes

1 teaspoon garam masala

1 teaspoon ground coriander

1/2 teaspoon ground turmeric

1/2 teaspoon sweet paprika

175g minced beef

1 tablespoon lemon juice

**1 tablespoon finely chopped
  fresh mint**

1 Cut 8cm-rounds from pastry. Place a level teaspoon of filling on one half of each round; brush edges with milk. Fold other pastry half over; press edges together to seal.

2 Heat oil in heated large wok or frying pan; deep-fry samosas until browned.

curried vegetable filling Heat oil in medium frying pan; cook onion, garlic and curry powder, stirring, until onion is soft. Stir in potato and carrot; cook, stirring 5 minutes or until vegetables are tender. Stir in peas. Remove from heat; cool.

meat filling Heat oil in large frying pan; cook onion, stirring, until browned lightly. Add garlic, ginger, chilli, garam masala and spices; cook, stirring, until fragrant. Add beef; cook, stirring, until well browned. Remove from heat. Stir in juice and mint; cool.

makes 30

per vegetable samosa 7.4g fat; 437kJ
per meat samosa 6.9g fat; 408kJ

tandoori chicken

PREPARATION TIME 20 MINUTES (plus marinating time) ■ COOKING TIME 1 HOUR 30 MINUTES

½ cup (150g) tandoori paste
1 cup (280g) yogurt
2 cloves garlic, crushed
2 teaspoons grated fresh ginger
1.6kg chicken
1 cup (250ml) green ginger wine

1 Combine paste, yogurt, garlic and ginger in large bowl; add chicken. Using hands, rub tandoori mixture all over chicken; refrigerate, covered, overnight.

2 Tuck chicken wings under body; tie legs together with kitchen string. Place chicken on oiled rack over baking dish. Pour wine into baking dish; bake, uncovered, in moderate oven about 1½ hours or until chicken is tender.

serves 6

per serving 26.6g fat; 1738kJ

pork vindaloo

PREPARATION TIME 20 MINUTES (plus standing time) ■ COOKING TIME 1 HOUR 30 MINUTES

1 tablespoon vegetable oil
1kg pork, cut into 3cm pieces
2 large brown onions (400g), sliced thinly
1 cup vegetable stock

vindaloo paste
2 teaspoons ground cumin
1 teaspoon chilli powder
2 teaspoons black mustard seeds
1½ teaspoons ground cinnamon
⅓ cup (80ml) white wine vinegar
1 teaspoon salt
1 teaspoon sugar
1 teaspoon ground cardamom
2 teaspoons ground turmeric
½ teaspoon ground cloves
1 teaspoon cracked black pepper
3 cloves garlic, crushed
1½ teaspoons ground ginger

mango sambal
1 medium mango (430g), chopped finely
1 fresh red thai chilli, chopped finely
1 tablespoon lemon juice
1 tablespoon finely chopped fresh mint

1 Heat oil in large saucepan; cook pork, in batches, until browned all over. Cook onion in pan, stirring, until soft.

2 Add vindaloo paste; cook, stirring, until fragrant. Add stock; return pork to pan. Bring to a boil.

3 Reduce heat to low; simmer, covered, stirring occasionally, about 1 hour or until pork is tender. Serve with mango sambal.

vindaloo paste Combine ingredients in small bowl; stand 30 minutes before using.

mango sambal Combine ingredients in small bowl. Cover; refrigerate at least 1 hour.

serves 4

per serving 15.4g fat; 1872kJ
tip Pork vindaloo can be made a day ahead and refrigerated, covered, or frozen for up to 3 months.

mixed **dhal**

PREPARATION TIME 10 MINUTES ■ COOKING TIME 1 HOUR 10 MINUTES

60g ghee

2 medium brown onions (300g), chopped finely

2 cloves garlic, crushed

1 tablespoon grated fresh ginger

1½ tablespoons black mustard seeds

1½ tablespoons ground cumin

1½ tablespoons ground coriander

2 teaspoons ground turmeric

¾ cup (150g) brown lentils

¾ cup (150g) red lentils

¾ cup (150g) yellow mung beans

¾ cup (150g) green split peas

800g canned tomatoes

1 litre (4 cups) vegetable stock

⅔ cup (160ml) coconut cream

¼ cup coarsely chopped fresh coriander

1 Heat ghee in large heavy-based saucepan; cook onion, garlic and ginger, stirring, until onion is soft. Add seeds and spices; cook, stirring, until fragrant.

2 Add lentils, beans and peas to pan; stir to combine. Add undrained crushed tomatoes and stock; bring to a boil. Reduce heat; simmer, covered, about 1 hour, stirring occasionally, until lentils are tender and mixture thickens. *[Can be frozen for up to 2 months.]*

3 Just before serving, add coconut cream and coriander; stir over low heat until heated through.

serves 8

per serving 14.3g fat; 1565kJ

tip If ghee is unavailable, clarify ordinary butter by heating it in small saucepan until white sediment comes to the surface; skim and discard sediment, and use the remaining heavy 'oil'.

bombay
potato masala

PREPARATION TIME 10 MINUTES ■ COOKING TIME 15 MINUTES

1.5kg potatoes

20g butter

1 large brown onion (200g), sliced thinly

3 cloves garlic, crushed

1 teaspoon yellow mustard seeds

3 teaspoons garam masala

2 teaspoons ground coriander

2 teaspoons ground cumin

½ teaspoon chilli powder

¼ teaspoon ground turmeric

400g canned tomatoes

1 Cut potatoes into wedges. Boil, steam or microwave potato until just tender; drain.

2 Heat butter in large frying pan; cook onion and garlic, stirring, until onion is soft. Add seeds and spices; cook, stirring, until fragrant.

3 Stir in undrained crushed tomatoes; cook, stirring, 2 minutes or until sauce thickens slightly. Add potato; gently stir until heated through.

serves 6

per serving 3.5g fat; 914kJ

vegetable curry
and paratha

PREPARATION TIME 50 MINUTES (plus standing time) ■ COOKING TIME 1 HOUR

1 tablespoon vegetable oil

2 medium brown onions (300g),
   chopped coarsely

2 cloves garlic, crushed

1 tablespoon black mustard seeds

2 teaspoons cumin seeds

1/2 teaspoon ground turmeric

1 tablespoon ground coriander

1/2 teaspoon ground cinnamon

2 large kumara (1kg),
   chopped coarsely

2 cups (500ml) vegetable stock

400g canned tomatoes

2 tablespoons tomato paste

11/2 cups (375ml) coconut milk

500g cauliflower, cut into florets

200g green beans, halved

600g canned chickpeas,
   rinsed, drained

1/4 cup coarsely chopped
   fresh coriander

paratha

5 medium potatoes (1kg),
   chopped coarsely

1/2 cup (100g) brown lentils

1 tablespoon vegetable oil

1 medium brown onion (150g),
   chopped coarsely

1 clove garlic, crushed

1 tablespoon black mustard seeds

2 teaspoons garam masala

1/4 cup coarsely chopped
   fresh coriander

3 cups (480g) wholemeal plain flour

3 cups (450g) plain flour

2 teaspoons salt

80g butter

2 cups (500ml) water, approximately

1 Heat oil in large saucepan; cook onion and garlic, stirring, until onion is soft. Add seeds and spices; cook, stirring, until fragrant. Add kumara; cook, stirring, 5 minutes.

2 Add stock, undrained crushed tomatoes and paste; bring to a boil. Reduce heat; simmer, uncovered, about 15 minutes or until kumara is almost tender. Stir in coconut milk and cauliflower; simmer, uncovered, 5 minutes. *[Can be frozen for up to 2 months.]*

3 Add beans and chickpeas; simmer, uncovered, about 10 minutes or until vegetables are tender. Just before serving, stir in coriander. Serve curry with paratha.

paratha Boil, steam or microwave potato until tender. Drain; mash until smooth. Cook lentils, uncovered, in small saucepan of boiling water about 15 minutes or until just tender; drain. Heat oil in small frying pan; cook onion and garlic, stirring, until onion is soft. Add seeds and garam masala; cook, stirring, until fragrant. Combine onion mixture in large bowl with potato, lentils and coriander. Place flours and salt in large bowl; rub in butter. Add enough of the water to form a soft dough; knead on floured surface about 10 minutes or until smooth and elastic. Cover with plastic wrap; stand 1 hour. Divide dough into 32 pieces; roll each piece on floured surface into a 14cm-round paratha. Layer paratha as they are rolled, separating each with plastic wrap to prevent them drying out. Spread 16 paratha on floured surface; divide potato filling among them, spreading to within 1cm of the edge. Brush edges of paratha with a little extra water; top each with one of the remaining paratha, pressing edges together to seal. Cook paratha on heated oiled grill plate (or grill or barbecue) until browned on both sides and heated through.

serves 8

per serving 28.7g fat; 3760kJ

lamb curry with cucumber raita

PREPARATION TIME 40 MINUTES ■ COOKING TIME 1 HOUR 10 MINUTES

1 medium eggplant (300g)

coarse cooking salt

1kg boned forequarter lamb, trimmed

2 medium potatoes (400g)

1 medium red capsicum (200g)

2 tablespoons vegetable oil

2 medium brown onions (300g),
   chopped coarsely

2 trimmed sticks celery (150g),
   chopped coarsely

2 cloves garlic, crushed

1 tablespoon grated fresh ginger

1/4 cup (75g) mild curry paste

425g canned tomatoes

1 cup (250ml) coconut milk

1 1/2 cups (300g) brown lentils

vegetable oil, for deep-frying

12 pappadums

cucumber raita

1 lebanese cucumber (130g),
   seeded, chopped finely

1 cup (280g) yogurt

1 clove garlic, crushed

1 Cut unpeeled eggplant into 2cm cubes; place in colander. Sprinkle all over with salt; stand 30 minutes to drain.

2 Meanwhile, cut lamb, potatoes and capsicum into 3cm pieces. Heat 1 tablespoon of the vegetable oil in large frying pan; cook lamb, in batches, until browned all over. Heat remaining oil in pan; cook onion, celery, garlic, ginger and paste, stirring until onion is soft.

3 Rinse eggplant well under cold running water; pat dry with absorbent paper. Combine eggplant with onion mixture in pan; add undrained crushed tomatoes, potato, capsicum and lamb. Stir until curry mixture comes to a boil; reduce heat. Simmer, covered, about 30 minutes or until lamb is just tender.

4 Add coconut milk to curry mixture; simmer, uncovered, further 10 minutes or until sauce thickens slightly.

5 Meanwhile, cook lentils in medium saucepan of boiling water, uncovered, about 10 minutes or until just tender. Drain lentils; cover to keep warm.

6 Heat vegetable oil in large frying pan. Cook pappadums, one at a time, until golden brown and puffed on both sides; turn with metal tongs. Drain pappadums on absorbent paper.

7 Serve lamb curry with lentils, pappadums and cucumber raita.

cucumber raita Combine ingredients in small bowl.

serves 4

per serving 49.3g fat; 4431kJ

coconut **pilaf**

PREPARATION TIME 10 MINUTES ■ COOKING TIME 35 MINUTES

60g ghee

2 medium brown onions (300g), sliced thinly

1 teaspoon cumin seeds

1 cinnamon stick

4 cardamom pods, bruised

3 whole cloves

1 teaspoon turmeric

1 cup (200g) basmati rice

1²/₃ cups (410ml) coconut cream

½ cup (125ml) water

½ cup (75g) pistachios, toasted, chopped coarsely

¼ cup (35g) currants

1 Melt ghee in large frying pan; cook onion, stirring over medium heat about 4 minutes or until soft. Stir in seeds, cinnamon, cardamom, cloves and turmeric; stir over medium heat 2 minutes.

2 Stir in rice; stir over heat a further minute. Stir in coconut cream and the water; bring to a boil. Reduce heat; simmer, covered, about 20 minutes or until all liquid is absorbed and rice is tender. Remove and discard cinnamon stick. Stir through nuts and currants. Stir pilaf with fork before serving.

serves 4

per serving 45.3g fat; 2757kJ

rogan josh

PREPARATION TIME 30 MINUTES (plus marinating time) ■ COOKING TIME 2 HOURS

1kg diced lamb

1 cup (280g) yogurt

1 tablespoon malt vinegar

4 cloves garlic, crushed

1 tablespoon grated fresh ginger

2 tablespoons ghee

4 cardamom pods, bruised

3 cloves

1 cinnamon stick

2 medium white onions (300g), chopped finely

3 teaspoons ground cumin

1 tablespoon ground coriander

1 teaspoon ground fennel

1½ teaspoons paprika

¾ teaspoon chilli powder

½ cup (125ml) chicken stock

1 teaspoon garam masala

2 tablespoons coarsely chopped fresh coriander

1 tablespoon finely chopped fresh mint

1 Combine lamb, yogurt, vinegar, half of the garlic and half of the ginger in large non-reactive bowl; mix well. Cover; refrigerate 3 hours or until required. *[Can be made a day ahead to this stage or frozen for up to a month.]*

2 Heat ghee in large saucepan; cook whole spices, stirring, until fragrant.

3 Add onion and remaining garlic and ginger; cook, stirring, until onion is browned lightly.

4 Add ground spices; cook, stirring, until fragrant. Add lamb mixture; stir to coat in spice mixture.

5 Add stock; simmer, covered, 1½ hours. Remove cover; simmer further 30 minutes or until lamb is tender. Just before serving, stir in garam masala and fresh herbs; heat through.

serves 6

per serving 16.4g fat; 1385kJ

tip Recipe can be made a day ahead and refrigerated, covered.

grilled nashi with rosewater syrup

PREPARATION TIME 10 MINUTES
COOKING TIME 15 MINUTES

2 cups (500ml) water
¾ cup (165g) caster sugar
2½ teaspoons rosewater
4 medium nashi (1kg), halved
1 tablespoon honey
1 tablespoon brown sugar

1 Combine the water, caster sugar and rosewater in medium saucepan; stir over heat, without boiling, until sugar dissolves. Add nashi; simmer, uncovered, about 10 minutes or until nashi is just tender.

2 Drain nashi over large heatproof bowl. Reserve syrup; cover to keep warm. Place nashi on oven tray. Drizzle with honey; sprinkle with brown sugar.

3 Grill nashi until sugar dissolves and nashi is browned lightly. Serve warm or cold with warm rosewater syrup.

serves 4

per serving 0.3g fat; 1339kJ.
tip Recipe can be made 3 hours ahead and refrigerated, covered.

lime and lemon grass mangoes

PREPARATION TIME 10 MINUTES
COOKING TIME 15 MINUTES

2 cups (440g) sugar
2 cups (500ml) water
1 tablespoon finely grated lime rind
¼ cup (60ml) lime juice
10cm piece fresh lemon grass, sliced thinly
2 kaffir lime leaves, sliced thinly
4 large mangoes (2.4kg)

1 Combine sugar, the water, rind, juice, lemon grass and lime leaves in medium saucepan. Stir over low heat until sugar dissolves; bring to a boil. Reduce heat; simmer, uncovered, about 15 minutes or until syrup thickens slightly.

2 Meanwhile, cut through mango lengthways, on each side of seed, to give two cheeks; peel away skin. Place mango in large heatproof bowl; pour syrup over mango. Serve warm or cold.

serves 4

per serving 0.9g fat; 2788kJ
tip Recipe can be made a day ahead and refrigerated, covered.

coconut topped papaya

PREPARATION TIME 10 MINUTES

- **2 medium red papaya (2kg), peeled, seeded, sliced thickly**
- **⅓ cup (80ml) lime juice**
- **2 passionfruit**
- **2 tablespoons flaked coconut, toasted**

1 Arrange papaya on large platter. *[Can be made 2 hours ahead to this stage and refrigerated, covered.]*

2 Drizzle with combined juice and passionfruit pulp; sprinkle coconut over top. Serve immediately.

serves 4

per serving 1.6g fat; 511kJ
tip Papaya are small red-fleshed pawpaws that are available from greengrocers who stock Asian ingredients.

pineapple wedges with palm sugar

PREPARATION TIME 15 MINUTES
COOKING TIME 5 MINUTES

- **1 medium pineapple (1.2kg), peeled**
- **60g palm sugar**

1 Cut pineapple into eight wedges; remove core from each. *[Can be made a day ahead to this stage and refrigerated, covered.]*

2 Place pineapple on oven tray; top each wedge with sugar. Cook under hot grill until sugar is melted and lightly golden (watch the sugar carefully as it melts much faster than white sugar). Serve immediately.

serves 8

per serving 0.1g fat; 243kJ

glossary

almonds, flaked blanched almonds shaved into paper-thin slices; keep refrigerated.

anchovies, dried also known as ikan bilis; available in packets from Asian food stores.

balmain bugs a type of sand lobster also known as shovelnose lobster or Moreton Bay bug; they taste like lobster, but the flesh is easier to remove from the shell. Substitute lobster if unavailable.

bamboo shoots the tender shoots of bamboo plants; available in cans.

banana leaves can be ordered from fruit and vegetable stores. Usually, one leaf is cut into about ten pieces. If you have a banana tree in your garden, cut leaf with a sharp knife close to the main stem then immerse in hot water so leaf will be pliable.

basil, thai also known as bai kaprow or holy basil; thai basil has small, crinkly leaves, purple stems and a strong, somewhat bitter, flavour. Most often used in stir-fries and curries. It is available from Asian food stores, and more recently, some supermarkets.

bay leaves aromatic leaves from the bay tree; use fresh or dried.

bean curd *see tofu*

bean sprouts also known as bean shoots; tender new growths of assorted beans and seeds germinated for consumption as sprouts. The most readily available are mung bean, soy bean, alfalfa and snow pea sprouts.

beans
packaged salted black soybeans which have been salted and fermented, they go particularly well with asparagus, broccoli and seafood. Chop or crush lightly before using.
peeled split mung also known as green gram or moong dhal; used widely in Asian cooking, either as beans – unhulled, hulled and split – or cooked to a paste and used in sweet dishes. Mung beans are widely used for sprouting.
snake long (about 40cm), thin, round green beans, with a taste similar to string beans and runner beans.

beef shin also known as gravy beef or boneless shin, it can also be purchased with the bone in. Shin is a slow-cooking cut perfect for stews and braises.

besan flour made from ground chickpeas; used to make the batter for Indian pakoras (fried vegetables).

bok choy *(bak choy, pak choi, chinese white cabbage, chinese chard)* mild, fresh mustard taste; use stems and leaves.
baby bok choy tender and more delicate in flavour.

bonito flakes, dried bonito is not a good eating fish, but when dried and shaved into flakes it is used, along with konbu (dried kelp) to make dashi.

breadcrumbs
japanese available in two types: fine crumbs and larger pieces. Both have a lighter texture than Western-style breadcrumbs.
packaged fine-textured, crunchy, purchased, white breadcrumbs. They will keep almost indefinitely, stored in an airtight container.
stale also called soft breadcrumbs; 1- or 2-day-old bread made into crumbs by grating, blending or processing. Can be frozen for up to 6 months.

cabbage, pickled mustard also known as gai choy, this cabbage is grown to be pickled. Available from Asian food stores.

candlenuts a hard, oily, slightly bitter nut, often ground and used to thicken Malaysian and Indonesian curries. Almonds, brazil nuts or macadamias can be substituted. Buy in small quantities and refrigerate to prevent the nuts becoming rancid.

cardamom seeds and pods native to India and used extensively in its cuisine, cardamom can be purchased in pod, seed or ground form. If using whole pods, bruise them lightly to release flavour. Cardamom has a distinctive aromatic, sweetly rich flavour and is one of the world's most expensive spices.

chilli
dried flakes dried red chillies that have been crushed, usually with the seeds (the seeds increases hotness). Store in a cool, dark place in an airtight container.
powder made from ground chillies, the Asian variety is the hottest; it can be used as a substitute for fresh chillies in the proportion of 1/2 teaspoon ground chilli powder to 1 medium chopped fresh chilli.

chillies

dried will vary in size and degree of heat, depending on which type has been dried (it is not usually specified). Soak in hot water until soft, then drain well before adding to dishes. Remove the seeds before soaking to reduce the fieriness, if preferred. The smaller the chilli, the hotter it is.

dutch (red & green) medium-hot, but flavourful, fairly long fresh chilli; sometimes referred to as a holland chilli.

red thai also called birdseye chillies, these tiny chillies are the hottest ones of all. They dry very well.

chinese barbecued pork also called char siew. Traditionally cooked in special ovens, this pork has a sweet-sticky coating made from soy sauce, sherry, five-spice powder and hoisin sauce. Available from Asian food stores.

chinese broccoli also known as gai lum and gai larn; leaves and stem are both eaten. Oyster sauce is the traditional Chinese accompaniment to gai larn.

chinese cabbage also known as peking cabbage or napa cabbage; resembles cos lettuce. It has a crisp texture and a milder, more delicate flavour than common cabbage.

chinese rice wine also known as Shaoxing wine; used in many Chinese dishes. Replace with a pale dry sherry, if unavailable. White wine or sake are not good substitutes.

chives, garlic these thick, flat, garlic-scented chives are stronger in flavour than the slender variety used in Western cooking. The plump flower bud is edible.

choy sum also known as flowering bok choy or flowering white cabbage. You can cook everything – leaves, flowers and stalks – although the Chinese prefer the stalks.

cinnamon an ingredient of five-spice powder and one of the fragrant spices commonly used in garam masala and other Indian spice mixes.

cloves, dried flower buds of a tropical tree; can be used whole or ground. A strong, fragrant spice used in Chinese five-spice powder and Indian garam masala.

coconut cream the first pressing from grated mature coconut and water.

coconut milk the second pressing (less rich) from grated mature coconut flesh; available in cans and cartons. A lower fat type (light coconut milk) is also sold.

coriander

dried coriander seeds and ground coriander must never be used to replace fresh coriander or vice versa. The tastes are completely different. Dried coriander

is a fragrant herb and one of the main ingredients in Indian curry blends.

fresh also known as cilantro and chinese parsley, coriander is the herb most often used in Asian cooking. In Thai food the whole plant is used – leaves, stems and roots. In Vietnam, India and China it's mostly the leaves.

cornflour also known as cornstarch; used as a thickening agent in cooking.

crab meat

canned quite bland in flavour, but convenient.

fresh buy live crabs if you can (blue swimmer and mud crabs have the best flavour). Freeze crabs for a few hours to immobilise them before cooking. Cook on the day of purchase.

picked the flesh of a cooked crab which has had all bits of cartilage removed; available fresh or frozen.

cucumber

lebanese small, slender and thin-skinned with juicy flesh and tiny seeds.

telegraph long and slender, also known as burpless or European cucumber.

cumin available both ground and as whole seeds; cumin has a warm, earthy, rather strong flavour and is especially important in Indian cooking.

curry leaves

fresh and dried buy fresh leaves at Indian food shops. Keep refrigerated, in a plastic bag, for a week or two; or dry out slowly in a very slow oven. Use leaves to give extra flavour and depth to curries; remove before serving just as you would bay leaves.

curry pastes there are many ready-made curry pastes on the market: madras, red thai, green thai, thai musaman, green masala paste, to mention a few. If you use them often, make your own curry pastes and store in clean, airtight jars in the refrigerator. There's no substitute for a good homemade curry paste. However, if you don't have time to make your own buy the best brand you can afford. Read the label to make sure the ingredients are authentic.

curry powder a blend of ground spices used for convenience when making Indian food. Can consist of some of the following spices in varying proportions: dried chilli, cinnamon, coriander, cumin, fennel, fenugreek, mace, cardamom and turmeric. Choose mild or hot to suit your taste and the recipe.

cuttlefish prepare cuttlefish in the same way as squid and octopus; cook it quickly to prevent toughening. Dried cuttlefish is available in some Asian shops and is eaten as a snack as is, or it can be reconstituted before cooking. Sarume is cuttlefish that has been seasoned and roasted.

daikon also called giant white radish; used liberally in Japanese cooking. It is said to aid digestion and cut the oiliness of foods, for example when it's finely grated and mixed into tempura dipping sauce.

dashi stock the all-purpose Japanese stock made from konbu and dried bonito flakes. Primary dashi, made from the first boiling of konbu and bonito, is used as a base for clear soups; secondary dashi, made from the konbu and bonito reserved from the first boiling, is used for thick soups and as a stock for cooking vegetables. Instant dashi is available in powder, granules and liquid concentrate.

eggplant also known as aubergine. Depending on their age, they may have to be sliced and salted to reduce their bitterness. Rinse and dry well before using.
baby also known as Japanese eggplant, these are small and slender. They don't need to be salted before use.

thai also known as pea eggplant, they are green and white, marble-sized and rather bitter.

fennel, seeds the fennel bulb isn't used in Asian cooking, but fennel seeds, whole and ground are used in the cooking of India, Malaysia and Indonesia. They have a strong aniseed flavour and are generally used in small quantities.

fenugreek seeds these bitter seeds are used sparingly in Indian curry mixtures.

five-spice powder a fragrant mixture of ground cinnamon, cloves, star anise, sichuan pepper and fennel seeds.

fu a Japanese specialty made of dried wheat gluten made into a spongy dough. It is made in a great variety of shapes. Soften in tepid water about 5 minutes before using.

galangal, fresh this is becoming easier to find outside specialist Asian shops. It looks like ginger but is dense and fibrous and much harder to cut than ginger. Galangal adds a distinctive flavour to anything it's used in, and is most often found in Thai, Malaysian and Singaporean food. If using in pieces, remove from the dish before serving.

Dried galangal is often called laos powder.

ghee clarified butter with the milk solids removed; can be heated to a high temperature without burning.

ginger
fresh also known as green or root ginger, an indispensable ingredient in almost all Asian cooking. Peeled ginger can be kept, covered with dry sherry in a jar and refrigerated or frozen in an airtight container.
pickled a palate cleanser in Japanese cuisine. Sweet and pink, pickled ginger is eaten with sushi and sashimi. Available in jars from specialty Asian food stores.

golden shallots *see onions*

garam masala a blend of spices, originating in north India; based on varying proportions of cardamom, cinnamon, cloves, coriander, fennel and cumin, roasted and ground together. Black pepper and chilli can be added for a hotter version.

gow gee wrappers little rounds of dough made from wheat flour and water. They are used to wrap around savoury fillings and then fried or steamed. Wonton wrappers can be substituted. Work with one wrapper at a time and keep the rest covered with a damp cloth to prevent them drying out.

green ginger wine alcoholic sweet wine with the taste of fresh ginger. In cooking, substitute dry (white) vermouth if you prefer, or even an equivalent amount of syrup from a jar of preserved ginger.

grenadine syrup a bright red non-alcoholic syrup made from pomegranate juice.

kaffir lime
leaves used liberally in Thai food, they impart a strong citrus flavour. Leaves are very thick and should be shredded finely and sprinkled over curries or added to salads. Dried leaves are also available; add these to curries.

rind the kaffir lime can be frozen. Remove from freezer when needed; grate a little of the rind, then replace in freezer in a plastic bag.

ketjap manis also called kecap manis, this is an Indonesian sweet, thick soy sauce which has sugar and spices added.

konbu also called kombu, this is dried kelp used, along with dried bonito flakes, to make the ubiquitous Japanese dashi stock. Konbu has a natural white-powder covering that shouldn't be rinsed off.

kumara Polynesian name of orange-fleshed sweet potato often confused with *yam*.

laksa paste a ready-made curry paste which contains spices, dried shrimp and peanuts. It is cooked with coconut milk and seafood or chicken to make Malaysian laksa. If difficult to obtain, replace with another medium-hot Malay-style curry paste.

lemon grass a tall, clumping, lemon-smelling and tasting, sharp-edged grass; only the white lower part of each stem is used.

lemon pepper seasoning a blend of crushed black pepper, lemon, herbs and spices.

lotus root the rhizome of the lotus plant; available frozen, dried or canned. It has a subtle flavour and crunchy texture and is used in the cooking of China, Japan, Thailand and India. Soak dried lotus root in hot water with a dash of lemon juice about 20 minutes before using.

lychees delicious juicy fruit, red-skinned, white-fleshed with a black seed. Eat just as they are or add to fruit salads. Also available canned in syrup.

macadamias rich, buttery nuts; store in refrigerator due to high oil content.

mint, vietnamese also known as laksa leaf. It is not a true mint and cannot be replaced in recipes with common mint; it has a sharp, pungent taste. As well as being used in laksa, it is often eaten raw in salads.

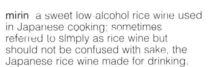

mirin a sweet low-alcohol rice wine used in Japanese cooking; sometimes referred to simply as rice wine but should not be confused with sake, the Japanese rice wine made for drinking.

miso fermented soybean paste. There are many types – generally the darker the miso, the saltier the taste and denser the texture. Used extensively in Japanese cooking for soups, sauces and dressings.

mushrooms

button small, cultivated white mushrooms with a delicate, subtle flavour.

shiitake also called chinese black mushrooms; used mainly in Chinese and Japanese cooking. They are fragrant and strongly flavoured. Available both dried and fresh. Soak dried mushrooms in hot water at least 20 minutes before using.

straw cultivated Chinese mushroom with earthy flavour; sold dried or canned in brine.

wood ear fungus known by many names including black fungus, cloud ear and tree ear, this fungus has little or no taste, but absorbs other flavours. It is used in Chinese cooking. Mostly sold dried, from Chinese shops; soak in water before use.

mustard seeds, black the hottest and most pungent of all mustard seeds; used in Indian cooking.

nashi also called japanese or asian pear, this sweet, juicy fruit has a similar taste to a pear but a much crisper texture.

harusame, dried very fine, white, almost transparent Japanese noodles. They are made from mung bean flour and are similar to bean thread noodles – use in the same way.

shirataki also called devil's tongue noodles, these are an ingredient in the Japanese dishes sukiyaki and shabu-shabu. Thin, translucent and jelly-like, they have a crunchy texture, but little flavour and are available fresh or dried. Keep fresh noodles refrigerated.

noodles

bean thread also called cellophane noodles or bean thread vermicelli; made from green mung bean flour. Soak before boiling, but not before frying.

hokkien also known as stir-fry noodles; fresh egg noodles resembling thick, yellow brown spaghetti needing no pre-cooking before being used.

soba made from buckwheat flour, these Japanese noodles are available frozen and dried.

rice stick these come in a variety of thicknesses and are also known as rice vermicelli. Soak in boiling water to soften 4 to 8 minutes, but test often because they can quickly turn mushy. Noodles can be deep-fried without prior soaking.

somen extremely thin dried wheat noodles from Japan; available fresh and dried from Japanese shops.

egg made from egg and wheat flour, these pale yellow noodles are sold in a range of widths. The noodles are dusted lightly with flour before packing to stop them sticking together; keep refrigerated.

green onions also known as scallion or (incorrectly) shallot; immature onions picked before the bulbs have formed; they have a long, bright-green edible stalk.

pandanus leaves especially popular in the cooking of Indonesia, Malaysia and Thailand; available fresh and dried in Asian food shops. Also called screwpine leaves and kewra.

oil
chilli made by steeping red chillies in vegetable oil; intensely hot in flavour.
peanut pressed from ground peanuts; most commonly used oil in Asian cooking because of its high smoke point.
sesame made from roasted, crushed, white sesame seeds; a flavouring rather than a cooking medium.
vegetable any of a number of oils sourced from plants rather than animal fats.

onions
fried bottled flakes of onion or shallots that have been deep-fried. Sprinkle over vegetables, noodles and rice.
golden shallots also called french shallots, these small, elongated, brown-skinned members of the onion family grow in tight clusters similar to garlic.

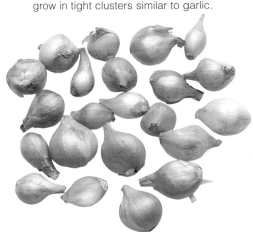

paprika ground dried red capsicum; available sweet or hot.

pawpaw large, pear-shaped red-orange tropical fruit. Sometimes used unripe (green) in cooking.

peppercorns
canned green the soft, unripe berry of the pepper plant, usually preserved in brine. Its flavour is less pungent than in its dried form.
sichuan these have a slightly numbing effect on the mouth and a clean, spicy fragrance; used extensively in Chinese cooking.

pipis small smooth-shelled triangular shaped bivalve mollusc. Clams can be substituted.

pork neck sometimes called pork scotch; an excellent roasting cut.

pork spare-ribs cut from the pork belly. Rich and fatty; excellent barbecued or grilled.

pork, chinese barbecued also known as char siew; roasted pork fillets with a sweet, sticky coating, available from Asian food stores.

prawn crackers large, pale crisp crackers. Enjoyed all over Asia; the best ones come from Indonesia.

quail small, delicate flavoured, domestically grown game bird ranging in weight from 250g to 300g.

rice noodle sheets fresh rice noodle sheets should be used on the day they are purchased. If this is not possible, refrigerate, covered, for a day. They will become hard, but will soften when cooked.

rice paper sheets are paper thin and made from a dough of rice flour, water and salt. Brush with water before use to make them pliable; while working with one sheet, keep remaining sheets covered in a damp tea-towel to prevent them drying out.

rice

basmati white, fragrant long-grained rice; should be washed several times before cooking.

jasmine aromatic long-grain white rice. White rice can be substituted but will not taste the same.

koshihikari small, round-grain white rice; grown in Australia from Japanese seed. Perfect for making sushi; available in supermarkets.

rosewater

extract made from crushed rose petals; called gulab in India. Used for its aromatic quality in many sweetmeats and desserts.

sake

Japan's favourite rice wine; used in cooking, marinading and as part of dipping sauces. If sake is unavailable, dry sherry, vermouth or brandy can be substituted. When consumed as a drink, it is served warm; stand the container in hot water about 20 minutes to warm the sake.

sambal oelek

(also ulek or olek) Indonesian in origin; a salty paste made from ground chillies.

sansho powder

also known as japanese pepper. A ground spice from the pod of the prickly ash; closely related to sichuan pepper.

sauce

black bean a Chinese sauce made from fermented soy beans, spices, water and wheat flour.

chinese barbecue a thick, sweet and salty commercial sauce used in marinades; made from fermented soy beans, vinegar, garlic, pepper and various spices. Available from Chinese specialty stores.

fish also called nam pla or nuoc nam; made from pulversised salted fermented fish, most often anchovies. Has a pungent smell and strong taste; use sparingly.

hoisin a thick, sweet and spicy Chinese paste made from salted fermented soy beans, onions and garlic.

hot chilli we used a Chinese variety made from chillies, salt and vinegar.

japanese soy also known as shoyu. Lighter and less salty than Chinese soy sauce. Always use Japanese soy sauce for Japanese cooking. Refrigerate after opening.

oyster a rich, brown sauce made from oysters and their brine, cooked with salt and soy sauce and thickened with starches.

plum a thick, sweet and sour dipping sauce made from plums, vinegar, sugar, chillies and spices.

soy made from fermented soy beans. Several varieties are available in most supermarkets and Asian food stores.
dark used for colour as well as flavour.
light light in colour but generally quite salty
sweet chilli mild, Thai sauce made from red chillies, sugar, garlic and vinegar.

sesame seeds

white sesame seeds are the most common, but black are also available. Black seeds have an earthier taste than the white. To toast, spread seeds evenly on oven tray, toast in moderate oven briefly.

seven-spice mix

also known as shichimi togarashi, it is made from chillies, sansho pepper, mandarin peel, white poppy seeds, dried seaweed (nori) and white sesame seeds. Used to season casseroles, soups and noodles.

shrimp paste

also known as trasi and blachan; a strong-scented, almost solid preserved paste made of salted dried shrimp. Used as a pungent flavouring in many Southeast Asian soups and sauces.

shrimps, dried

available at Asian food shops in plastic packets. Once opened, store in the refrigerator. Use fried and sprinkled over vegetables and noodle dishes, or add to stir-fries and soups as a flavour boost.

sichuan seasoning

powdered mix of garlic, salt, ginger, paprika, onion, pepper, chives, red pepper and spices.

snow pea sprouts

sprouted seeds of the snow pea. Use in salads and as a garnish.

soy bean paste

made from fermented soy beans. Several variations are available in most supermarkets and Asian food stores.

spring roll wrappers

are also sometimes called egg roll wrappers; they come in various sizes and can be purchased fresh or frozen from Asian supermarkets. Made from a delicate wheat-based pastry; can be used for making gow gees and samosas as well as spring rolls.

star anise a dried star-shaped pod whose seeds have an astringent aniseed flavour.

su

(sushi rice vinegar) a blend of japanese rice vinegar, sugar and salt used especially to make sushi rice; also used as a dressing for sunomono (vinegared food). Available in Asian markets and most larger supermarkets.

sugar

brown a soft, fine sugar retaining molasses.

palm also known as jaggery, jawa and gula melaka; from the coconut palm. Dark brown to black in colour; usually sold in rock-hard cakes. The sugar of choice in most Asian cooking.

tamarind concentrate

a thick, purple-black, ready-to-use paste extracted from the pulp of the tamarind bean; used as is, with no soaking, stirred into sauces and casseroles to add a sour flavour.

tat soi also known as rosette pak choy, tai gu choy and chinese flat cabbage, it is a tender variety of bok choy.

tofu also known as bean curd, tofu is a bland, slightly nutty food made from soy bean "milk". Its neutral taste gives it the ability to absorb the flavours of the food with which it is cooked. Readily available from supermarkets in water-packed containers. Once opened, store in the refrigerator in water for a few days at most. Change the water daily. There are several types of tofu.

firm this has been pressed slightly; it holds its shape and can be cut into cubes.

fried small cubes of firm tofu already deep-fried until the surface is brown and crusty and the inside almost dry; can be purchased ready for use.

prepared fried bean curd pockets of bean curd (tofu) which are able to be opened out to take a filling. Available from Asian food stores.

silken custard-like, soft, white tofu, much used in Japanese cooking.

tempeh not actually tofu, tempeh is made from fermented soy beans which become solid. It can be sliced or cut into cubes and steamed, baked or fried. Or it can be blended into a dip.

turmeric a member of the ginger family, its root is dried and ground, resulting in the thick yellow powder that gives many Indian dishes their characteristic colour. It is intensely pungent in taste but not hot.

vinegar
malt made from fermented malt and beech shavings.
red wine made from fermented red wine.
rice made from fermented rice; colourless and flavoured with sugar and salt. Also known as seasoned rice vinegar.
rice wine made from rice wine lees (sediment), salt and alcohol.

wakame a deep green, edible seaweed popular in Japan. It has the fresh taste of the sea and is used in soups and simmered dishes. Wakame is available both in fresh and dried forms in Asian food shops. Soften dried wakame in cold water before cooking briefly.

wasabi an Asian horseradish used to make a fiery sauce traditionally served with Japanese raw fish dishes; sold in powdered or paste form.

water chestnuts resemble chestnuts in appearance, hence the English name. They are small brown tubes with a crispy white, nutty-tasting flesh. Their crunchy texture is best experienced fresh, however canned water chestnuts are more easily obtained and can be refrigerated for a month after opening.

wonton wrappers gow gee, egg or spring roll pastry sheets can be substituted.

wood ear fungus *see mushrooms.*

yabbies a small freshwater crayfish often bred in dams. Cook as for other crustaceans.

index

facts and figures

Wherever you live, you'll be able to use our recipes with the help of these easy-to-follow conversions. While these conversions are approximate only, the difference between an exact and the approximate conversion of various liquid and dry measures is but minimal and will not affect your cooking results.

dry measures

metric	imperial
15g	1/2oz
30g	1oz
60g	2oz
90g	3oz
125g	4oz (1/4lb)
155g	5oz
185g	6oz
220g	7oz
250g	8oz (1/2lb)
280g	9oz
315g	10oz
345g	11oz
375g	12oz (3/4lb)
410g	13oz
440g	14oz
470g	15oz
500g	16oz (1lb)
750g	24oz (1 1/2lb)
1kg	32oz (2lb)

liquid measures

metric	imperial
30ml	1 fluid oz
60ml	2 fluid oz
100ml	3 fluid oz
125ml	4 fluid oz
150ml	5 fluid oz (1/4 pint/1 gill)
190ml	6 fluid oz
250ml	8 fluid oz
300ml	10 fluid oz (1/2 pint)
500ml	16 fluid oz
600ml	20 fluid oz (1 pint)
1000ml (1 litre)	1 3/4 pints

helpful measures

metric	imperial
3mm	1/8in
6mm	1/4in
1cm	1/2in
2cm	3/4in
2.5cm	1in
5cm	2in
6cm	2 1/2in
8cm	3in
10cm	4in
13cm	5in
15cm	6in
18cm	7in
20cm	8in
23cm	9in
25cm	10in
28cm	11in
30cm	12in (1ft)

helpful measures

The difference between one country's measuring cups and another's is, at most, within a 2 or 3 teaspoon variance. (For the record, 1 Australian metric measuring cup holds approximately 250ml.) The most accurate way of measuring dry ingredients is to weigh them. When measuring liquids, use a clear glass or plastic jug with the metric markings. (One Australian metric tablespoon holds 20ml; one Australian metric teaspoon holds 5ml.)

Note: North America, NZ and the UK use 15ml tablespoons. All cup and spoon measurements are level.

We use large eggs having an average weight of 60g.

how to measure

When using graduated metric measuring cups, shake dry ingredients loosely into the appropriate cup. Do not tap the cup on a bench or tightly pack the ingredients unless directed to do so. Level top of measuring cups and measuring spoons with a knife. When measuring liquids, place a clear glass or plastic jug with metric markings on a flat surface to check accuracy at eye level.

oven temperatures

These oven temperatures are only a guide. Always check the manufacturer's manual.

	°C (Celsius)	°F (Fahrenheit)	Gas Mark
Very slow	120	250	1
Slow	150	300	2
Moderately slow	160	325	3
Moderate	180 - 190	350 - 375	4
Moderately hot	200 - 210	400 - 425	5
Hot	220 - 230	450 - 475	6
Very hot	240 - 250	500 - 525	7

Sub-editor *Debbie Quick*
Designer *Alison Windmill*
Special feature photographer *Scott Cameron*
Special feature stylist *Sarah O'Brien*

Test Kitchen Staff
Food editor *Pamela Clark*
Associate food editor *Karen Hammial*
Assistant food editors *Kirsty McKenzie, Louise Patniotis*
Home economists *Clare Bradford, Emma Braz,*
Kimberley Coverdale, Kelly Cruickshanks,
Sarah Hobbs, Amanda Kelly, Alison Webb
Test kitchen manager *Elizabeth Hooper*
Editorial co-ordinator *Juliet Ingersoll*

Home Library Staff
Editor-in-chief *Mary Coleman*
Managing editor *Susan Tomnay*
Senior writer and editor *Georgina Bitcon*
Senior editor *Liz Neate*
Chief sub-editor *Julie Collard*
Sub-editor *Debbie Quick*
Art director *Michele Withers*
Designers *Mary Keep, Caryl Wiggins, Alison Windmill*
Studio manager *Caryl Wiggins*
Editorial coordinator *Holly van Oyen*
Book sales manager *Jennifer McDonald*

Chief executive officer *John Alexander*
Group publisher *Jill Baker*
Publisher *Sue Wannan*

Produced by *The Australian Women's Weekly*
Home Library, Sydney.
Colour separations by ACP Colour Graphics Pty Ltd,
Sydney. Printing by Dai Nippon, Hong Kong.
Published by ACP Publishing Pty Limited,
54 Park St, Sydney; GPO Box 4088, Sydney, NSW 1028.
Ph: (02) 9282 8618 Fax: (02) 9267 9438.
awwhomelib@acp.com.au
www.awwbooks.com.au

AUSTRALIA: Distributed by Network Distribution
Company, GPO Box 4088, Sydney, NSW 1028.
Ph: (02) 9282 8777 Fax: (02) 9264 3278.
UNITED KINGDOM: Distributed by Australian
Consolidated Press (UK), Moulton Park Business Centre,
Red House Rd, Moulton Park, Northampton, NN3 6AQ
Ph: (01604) 497 531 Fax: (01604) 497 533
acpukltd@aol.com
CANADA: Distributed by Whitecap Books Ltd, 351 Lynn Ave,
North Vancouver, BC, V7J 2C4, Ph: (604) 980 9852.
NEW ZEALAND: Distributed by Netlink Distribution
Company, Level 4, 23 Hargreaves St, College Hill,
Auckland 1, Ph: (9) 302 7616.
SOUTH AFRICA: Distributed by PSD Promotions (Pty) Ltd,
PO Box 1175, Isando 1600, SA, Ph: (011) 392 6065, and
CNA Limited, Newsstand Division, PO Box 10799,
Johannesburg 2000, SA, Ph: (011) 491 7500.

Great Asian Food.
Includes index.
ISBN 1 86396 239 5
1. Cookery, Asian. 2. Cookery, Oriental. 3. Vegetarian
cookery. I. Title: Australian Women's Weekly.
(Series: Australian Women's Weekly Home Library).
641.595

© ACP Publishing Pty Limited 2001
ABN 18 053 273 546

Photographers: *Alan Benson, Kevin Brown, Scott Cameron,*
Robert Clark, Gerry Colley, Rowan Fotheringham,
Louise Lister, Mark O'Meara, Rob Shaw, Robert Taylor,
Jon Waddy, Ian Wallace.

Stylists: *Jon Allen, Myles Beaufort, Wendy Berecry, Clare Bradford,*
Marie-Helene Clauzon, Jane Collins, Rosemary de Santis,
Georgina Dolling, Carolyn Fienberg, Kay Francis, Jane Hann,
Trish Heagerty, Jacqui Hing, Cherise Koch, Victoria Lewis,
Vicki Liley, Janet Mitchell, Michelle Noerianto, Sarah O'Brien,
Anna Phillips, Jenny Wells, Sophia Young.

Cover: Shellfish Laksa, page 140
Photographer: Ian Wallace
Stylist: Sarah O'Brien

Back cover: Beef and pork satays, page 166
Photographer: Scott Cameron
Stylist: Sarah O'Brien